Jan's refreshing tell-the-truth style—
and friend—instantly drew me to
to where the pancake hits the griddle. She's not afraid of
the heat in life, whether it shows up as aging, grief, or
a scorching heartbreak. Her well-researched material will
feed your soul and help equip you for the season you're in.
It has for me. This is a knapsack book to accompany us on
the journey. Thanks, Jan.

PATSY CLAIRMONT
Speaker and author of *You Are More Than You Know*

We live in a culture that seems to be in denial about getting
older. As boomers inch toward retirement years, we tend
to think of seniors as "them" and not "us." In *Courage for
the Unknown Season*, Jan Silvious, in her trusted voice, puts
getting older into beautiful perspective. Whatever season
you're in, Jan's words of wisdom will help you embrace
every moment as a gift from God.

BABBIE MASON
Award-winning singer-songwriter, speaker, and author of
Embraced by God

Jan Silvious has a steady perspective on life! She is open and
real and can relate. This new book gives us a big dose of
practical wisdom for trusting God today and in the days to
come—and to even laugh at the future. Jan encourages us
to squeeze out life's joys to make a difference for ourselves
and others we love.

DEBBIE PETERSEN
Missionary with Campus Crusade for Christ (Cru) for 34 years

Wisdom is defined as skill in godly living. *Courage for the Unknown Season* abounds with practical wisdom for living in today's world while being aware of the necessity of preparing for our next unknown season. *Relevant, down to earth*, and *engaging* describe Silvious's book; it deserves to be on everyone's bucket list. Be challenged and encouraged as you "head toward ninety"!

CYNTHIA HEALD,
Speaker and author of the Becoming A Woman of . . . Bible study series

Intellect. Wisdom. Depth. Faith. Wit. Jan Silvious is an extraordinary communicator who has once again combined all of these, and the result is a remarkable gift to all of us. Part research scientist, part life coach, part big sis, Jan serves up powerful, practical, and proven insights to guide us toward our final destination. This is a must-read for those who want a GPS for the unpredictable road ahead. In Jan's most personal book to date, we are granted the privilege of gleaning from a well-loved woman and her well-lived life. In these times of fear and doubt, we absolutely need *Courage for the Unknown Season*.

ELLIE LOFARO
Author, international speaker, Bible teacher

COURAGE

for the

UNKNOWN

SEASON

*Navigating What's Next
with Confidence and Hope*

JAN SILVIOUS

A NavPress resource published in alliance
with Tyndale House Publishers, Inc.

NavPress is the publishing ministry of The Navigators, an international Christian organization and leader in personal spiritual development. NavPress is committed to helping people grow spiritually and enjoy lives of meaning and hope through personal and group resources that are biblically rooted, culturally relevant, and highly practical.

For more information, visit www.NavPress.com.

Courage for the Unknown Season: Navigating What's Next with Confidence and Hope
Copyright © 2017 by Jan Silvious. All rights reserved.

A NavPress resource published in alliance with Tyndale House Publishers, Inc.

NAVPRESS is a registered trademark of NavPress, The Navigators, Colorado Springs, CO. The NAVPRESS logo is a trademark of NavPress, The Navigators. *TYNDALE* is a registered trademark of Tyndale House Publishers, Inc. Absence of ® in connection with marks of NavPress or other parties does not indicate an absence of those marks.

The Team:
Don Pape, Publisher
Caitlyn Carlson, Acquisitions Editor
Ron C. Kaufmann, Designer

Cover photograph of birds copyright © Justin Lewis/MediaBakery. All rights reserved.

Author photograph by Renita & Kerry Friesen, MD, copyright © 2016. All rights reserved.

Published in association with The Blythe Daniel Agency, Inc., P.O. Box 64197, Colorado Springs, CO 80962.

Some of the anecdotal illustrations in this book are true to life and are included with the permission of the persons involved. All other illustrations are composites of real situations, and any resemblance to people living or dead is purely coincidental.

For information about special discounts for bulk purchases, please contact Tyndale House Publishers at csresponse@tyndale.com, or call 1-800-323-9400.

Cataloging-in-Publication Data is available.

ISBN 978-1-63146-788-2

Printed in the United States of America

24	23	22	21	20
8	7	6	5	4	3

*To my sister-friends who have blessed me with your love and
unfailing support: How can I say thank you for your many
kindnesses? Without "we" there would be no "me"!*

---

*To my husband, Charlie, who abides forever faithful:
Over fifty summers have come and gone since we became husband
and wife. We entered the unknown together, and here we are
a half century later, all the better for the wear!*

---

*To my sons—David, Jon, and Aaron:
You are fine men, and no mama could be more proud!
The seasons we shared growing up together were
some of the best in my life!*

---

*To my daughters-in-love, Sandi and Heather:
You are both special in such different and wonderful ways.
I'm so glad my sons had sense enough to marry you!*

---

*To my grandchildren—Lauren, Luke, Rachel, Ben, and Bekah:
You have adorned my winter season with your beautiful selves!
I have loved you in all your seasons, and I always will.*

CONTENTS

CHAPTER ONE

SEASONS COME AND SEASONS GO

———— ∞∞ ————

The Moving Finger writes; and, having writ,
Moves on: nor all thy Piety nor Wit
Shall lure it back to cancel half a Line,
Nor all thy Tears wash out a Word of it.

OMAR KHAYYAM

I WAS RUMMAGING through an old hope chest when I came upon a stack of crispy and yellowed papers. I recognized the construction paper hearts and stick-pencil sketches immediately—the awkward drawings and rhyming poems of my children, all preserved with the full intent of keeping them safe forever. Storing these papers in this chest had been my "busy-mother filing system." It was as if I had the wispy dream that I could hold on to my children by holding on to their artwork and scribbled words. But wishful thinking doesn't hold back the days or years.

My children have been grown a long time now. In fact,

they've been gone so long that their children are beginning the leaving process. So it goes. Season has followed season, and here we are—the littles, the middles, and the olders all living in seasons that won't stop changing. We all are living in a world we experience uniquely, becoming who we are and who we will be.

That is the nature of life. For the most part, these changing seasons seem right, but when we find ourselves moving from a season we've loved into a season we're not so sure we'll like, it can be a challenge to find the strength, will, and just plain courage to keep going. It's often been said, "Old age isn't for sissies," but I can tell you, there's no place for "sissy living" in many of the seasons of life.

Seasonal changes start early. Leaving the womb catapults us into a world of incredible challenges. Childhood is touted as carefree, but not every stage of childhood is welcomed! Some come with great awkwardness and emotional angst, but each stage is necessary to become the adults we long to be.

And, too, there are victories to be celebrated with each milestone we face. I laughed out loud when one of my granddaughters observed her pimple-free face in the mirror and declared, "Puberty has been kind to me!" She had traversed a worrisome, pimply season toward adulthood, and she had won!

But as we grow toward and through adulthood, sometimes the seasons bring concerns we haven't faced before.

Relationships become more intense and more significant. Marriages, good or bad, start, continue, or sometimes break up. No matter what happens, life is never the same. We are constantly changing, and the confident choices made at twenty can become the heart pangs of forty. The "happily ever after" at the altar can become the "never any longer." I've learned over the years that it's impossible to make a perfect decision because we don't know the future. Marriages don't always work out, singleness isn't always as free as you thought it would be, and life is always full of surprises. So leaning into each season and learning its lesson is one of the gifts of living. And there are many gifts in this life!

If you welcome children into your family, no amount of preparation matters—no one can adequately describe the pangs of childbirth and the exhilaration of hearing that first cry. You will wear that child on your heart for the rest of your days and through unknown seasons, through incredible highs and terrifying lows, through overwhelming joy and wrenching concern. Each day goes back and forth between *Isn't he amazing?* and *Whose kid is that?*

One minute you've baked your last cupcake for a homeroom party, and then, before you turn around, your sixteen-year-old is leaving the driveway in a car that is way too big and powerful for her. Yet to deny her that privilege is to deny her the very essence of her life—growing up! It's a season of "one last time."

So while you are living in these times,
remember there are only so many of them,
and when they are gone,
you will yearn for just one more day of them.
For one last time.

AUTHOR UNKNOWN

Then you watch the twentysomethings fall in love, fall out of love, struggle with who they are, and wonder who they will become. Watching helplessly, without interference or subtle manipulation, is hard. Your children have to make life decisions on their own. It's tough to watch, but it's a season.

Children become adults, have their own children, and take jobs in what might as well be a foreign country, where they succeed royally or sometimes fail miserably. Time marches forward. The changing of seasons is relentless.

Meanwhile comes that season of caring for aging parents. Watching the people who have always been there begin to fade and become weaker or slower is a season we would all like to skip over. Seeing their decline sometimes takes you by surprise. "When did this begin?" you ask. "They were fine last summer." You didn't see it coming—or maybe you did and it was just easier to look away. Unexpected and often unwanted obligations fall on your shoulders for an unknown amount of time. Your parents are now the lightweights, and you have become the heavyweight. You bear the major responsibility for their care. This is a season of juggling careers, traveling back and forth, and managing. There's no way around this difficult and unknown season.

If you have children, you can find yourself being stretched between the ailing eighty-year-old in another state and the needy eighteen-year-old under your roof. You are sandwiched between them, pulled to give each of them more and yet incapable of giving either of them enough. Your own needs are sublimated for what seems like a long time, but soon enough the generational squeeze changes, and you're left with sorrow tangled with joy. The young one is flying from the nest, and he will be missed. The old one is flying from a body wracked with pain. With great heaviness, you've urged her to go, whispering, "It's okay. We'll all be fine." Unbelievably, she breathes her last, and then she, too, will be missed oh so very much.

Whether you've handled this difficult season while trying to maintain a corporate career or trying to maintain a home—or both—you are left drained and a little bewildered. The season of good-byes is hard, although death after suffering often brings relief and a sad joy that your parent is free from that frail, used-up body. Another season has come to a close, and you find yourself older, wiser, and wondering, *Now what?*

You may not feel old enough to be in this season. You may not be. Hard leavings and parents' dying can occur at any age. Whenever it happens, you're catapulted into a new season. It seems like spring was just yesterday, and yet you feel the chill of winter. How did you get here? Summer came and went, and so did fall. The unknown seasons can seem like long shadows across a cold, snowy landscape. What's next? Will the sun shine? Will it warm up, or are we in for a hard freeze? Winter can be such a changeable time, and the unknowable aspect of change can rattle our confidence and shake our hope.

No matter our age, we all face seasons of change, and change can be so hard to embrace. Even if the change takes you into a season you love, the unknown is always a little unsettling. Not every day is the same. Not every change will unfold the same way.

I love the springtime, but I live in tornado country, so I know that in the midst of warm air and budding trees, horrific storms can blow up without much warning. That's sort of the way our lives are. Even if you have no idea what the seasonal change will bring, however, you can face it with courage: You can prepare as much as possible and recognize that the change doesn't have to be the end. It could well be the beginning of some new discovery, a new relationship, or an adventure you never dreamed of having. In fact, many times we miss God's promise to those who love Him (who are in a relationship with Him) that He "causes all things" (even unknown seasons) "to work together for good for those who love God, to those who are called according to His purpose" (Romans 8:28).

Learning from Other Generations

Facing the unknown season feels terrifying, but it doesn't have to be. Sometimes all we need is a little perspective. We can forget that we are part of a generation—and that our generation can have a profound influence on how we view the changes of life. Learning from the other generations around us—older and younger—can have an amazing impact.

There are five generations of people living together on the earth right now, and you and I are connected to millions of other people through one of those generations.[1] These different age groups are doing life together while melding their age perspectives, cultural influences, and personal worldviews into their life experiences.

No wonder we shake our heads at times when we consider the generation that came before us and the one that follows us. Each generation has its own unique brand, and we will naturally have an affinity for the one in which we were born. We all think our own generation is the smartest, is most "with it," and has the most to offer.

We also seem to allow a kindly tolerance for generations once removed from ourselves (think grandparents and grandchildren). We may give those generations a little more slack and kind acceptance for their deficits and peculiarities.

Our generational biases mean that we primarily like to connect with people with whom we have a shared history.

We "get" our generation. Certain songs stir in our collective memory. Certain dates like December 7 or November 22 or September 11 trigger profound memories of where we were when we heard the news of that day.[2]

As a baby boomer, I have a lot of generational memories lingering in my head. I'm sure that's also true of the other seventy-six million of us. We connect because we were born during those years between 1946 and 1964, and we came of age to the same music and the same cultural heroes and tragedies: We cut our musical teeth on rock and roll and the Beatles. We saw civil rights change dramatically. We experienced the shock of the assassinations of President John Kennedy, his brother Bobby Kennedy, and the Reverend Martin Luther King, Jr. And we lived our young lives tormented by the war in Vietnam—albeit with a freer, more self-indulgent view of life than our parents' generation had.

They are called the silent generation. They hit the planet between 1927 and 1945 and were greatly impacted by their experiences of the Great Depression and World War II. They were highly moral and took commitment to marriage seriously. Divorce was initially uncommon. However, in later years their divorce rate began to rise, leading to high divorce rates among boomers as well. Boomers were known for doing things differently, and their approach to marriage, divorce, work, and retirement was not going to be like anyone else's before or after them.

The silent generation saw great virtue in staying with the same company throughout their entire careers, whereas the boomers, the gen Xers who followed, and the millennials after them have viewed "company loyalty" as a oxymoron. The silent generation worked their lifetimes at the same company, if they were lucky, for a retirement that meant a rocking chair, peace, and a decent pension. I still can hear my dad, who worked at the same job for thirty years, saying, "All I want is peace, quiet, and money." As a boomer, I used to giggle and think, *That's the last thing on earth I want—except maybe the money!*

The subsequent generations have modified the boomers' hefty divorce rate. Many of them were traumatized by their boomer parents' divorces and remarriages, so they have become more cautious and age delayed when it comes to their own marriages. In fact, they also have made cohabitation more acceptable, a thought that would have been scandalous to the silent generation and not that well accepted by most aging boomers.

The millennials are also known as the "echo boomers" because they are almost as many in number as the boomers. They have been highly nurtured by hovering parents and have never known a world without computers. They tend to discount the authority of older generations, believing authority is earned not by tenure but by competency. And they find that social hierarchies get in the way of creative collaboration, which they highly value. Their favorite forms of expression include tattoos and body art, and the thought of being with one company for a lifetime gives them the jitters.

In 2006, children were born in record numbers, setting off a "baby boomlet." This new generation far outnumbers the starting numbers for the boomers and the millennials. They have been raised on computers and are sometimes tagged with the identity KGOY—"Kids Getting Older Younger." They are affecting the economy as their interest in toys dwindles and their interest in computers and computer games grows. And the economy may not be all that is affected. As your children, grandchildren, or great-grandchildren, they will relate to you who came later to the computer age differently from how they will relate to their peers and their whole environment. This is the "remains to be seen" generation. Right now, it's anyone's guess as to how their interactions with electronics will fundamentally change who they are and how they relate.

Just being born in one of these generations does not pigeonhole you with the characteristics I've mentioned, but understanding our generation will help us see why we view the world as we do. Believe it or not, the generation you were born in will have a great deal of influence on what your seasons will look like, because each of the five generations living together on the earth right now has a different way of doing life. As you find yourself among the generations, think about your life experience in relationship to the current culture and ask yourself why the world might be feeling a little strange to you now. Changes come in culture as well as in our personal lives, and keeping our equilibrium as things change around us is part of learning to live in new seasons.

Even this quick look at the generations should give us insight into the seasonal changes we all face. Many more changes will come, and the differences among our mind-sets mean that the seasonal forecast for each generation will vary. For some, warm spring breezes are blowing; wintry blasts chill others. Not all changes are negative—they are just different. Knowing our generational and cultural differences can give us the wisdom and insight to approach life and connection with a strong spirit rather than with fear or dread.

Milestones

The boomers hit a milestone in 2016, when the oldest turned seventy. I find myself among them, but I continue to think of myself as fifty. That was such a comfortable, solid age—postmenopausal and prearthritic. It seemed like a great place to hunker down, so that's what I've done in my mind. The thought that I'm in my seventies sets me back. I recoil—I can't be that age! "Seventy" sounds so old. I don't feel old, I don't think old, and I make every effort not to act old.

Now, seventy may or may not be old to you, depending on your age and place in a society that has mixed views on aging. A survey by the Pew Research Center revealed the following:

> Perceptions of the onset of old age varied widely according to the respondent's age. People under 30 believe that old age strikes before the average person turns 60, whereas middle-aged respondents said that old age begins at 70 and adults aged 65 or older put the threshold closer to 74.
>
> Gender made a difference in the findings too. On average, women said that a person becomes old at age 70, whereas men said that the magic number is closer to 66 years of age.[3]

You will read this book with your own perspective on the seasons of life, depending on where you are. If you are in your twenties, thirties, or forties, I know you'll have no place to put the number seventy in your head. You've never been there, and most of the people you know who are seventy seem so far removed from your world. Those of us who are there understand. Seventy seemed like a faraway place to us, too, when we were young.

I asked my good friend Patsy Clairmont, who is seventy-one, "How did you see people in the sixty-to-eighty age group when you were in your twenties?" In typical Patsy fashion, she said, "I saw them like they were tottering their way home. They sometimes smelled funny, their clothes seemed untidy, and they were somewhat withdrawn. They also seemed out of touch with world changes." I laughed at Patsy's comment but remembered feeling the same way. I only vaguely knew one of my grandmothers. She died at seventy-three, but I do remember her black lace-up shoes, rimless glasses, white bun, and pastel housedress. She was of the generation Patsy was talking about.

Although there's a great generational and philosophical divide today, we can learn much from one another. No matter what season you're in, you will need courage for what's next. God keeps the curtain to the future closed. Rarely does He ever give us a peek into that which is to come. So no matter our age, we will walk into situations where we'll need courage to navigate what's coming. One source of courage comes from having the mind-set to learn from people who have already walked these roads. What can they teach us? And what can we learn from those who are coming behind? May I say, there is much to be learned from both ways.

I have regular conversations with a group of millennials. I love talking with them. They are primarily focused on what they will become, where their romantic lives will settle, and what's happening in their world. Sometimes we'll chat about the past, and when I mention events that happened in the sixties, they giggle with wonder that I was alive then! They're even more in awe that when I was their age, I was already married and the mother of three. We usually have a good laugh at their disbelief and then move on to what they are interested in. I love hearing what and how they think. I can look back and engage my twenty-year-old mind and relate to so much that they say, but in my more seasoned mind, I can see some things that might be helpful to them.

Tattoos always make a good point of discussion with my younger buddies. If I spot a tattoo on someone, I always ask what story their tattoo is telling, and they readily tell me exactly what they're trying to communicate. I met a young woman on the plane who had tattoos covering the whole length of her arm. She was young, smart, and beautiful. When I asked her what her tattoo story was, she said, "It's the novel I've just written." Then she began to show me the characters and their connections, tattooed from her shoulder to the back of her hand. She was thrilled that I had asked. She wanted to tell me about her writing, and this was her way!

The millennial love for that form of self-expression is becoming legendary, and yet it seems so foreign to a boomer. Often I ask people how long they've had their tattoos and how they feel about them being so permanent. They think nothing of pointing to some and saying, "I wish I didn't have these," but in the same breath they might say, "I want to get this new artist's work on my back!" I listen with seventy-year-old ears and think, *Yikes!*

While the generations can enjoy one another's conversations, in the long run we are in danger of being like children on a playground, quickly settling into cliques—bonding with people our own age and in our own stage of life because we have a kind of "knowing" between us. We find our own people because we share memories and experiences that can't be repeated.

When my generation connects with younger generations, we're sometimes prone to talk about how we did things and how different things are now. As one woman told me recently, "I've learned not to tell my millennial daughter how I raised her. I've tried to tell her that she did okay in spite of all the things I did that she wouldn't dream of doing with her baby now. She doesn't want to hear it. She told me I had to take a CPR course before she'd let me watch her baby! Can you imagine?" Yes, I can imagine. But if it means being able to keep our grandbabies, it's worth humbling ourselves to accommodate millennial parenting styles. We can't miss these relationships because we're too proud to enter them.

We also don't want to miss the value of cross-generational connection. Often that's a pride issue too. When we say we have "nothing in common," we're really saying, "It's just too hard to connect." Olders sometimes think they won't know how to talk to youngers, and youngers think olders don't care what they think. But if we just take the first step toward one another, we might be amazed at what we can learn.

Lexi is a twenty-three-year-old friend of mine who showed up in my world because she wanted to learn something about what I do as a life coach, speaker, and writer. That's her aspiration! She contacted me, we met, we began to talk, and we've been chatting ever since. Our times together are no longer just confined to her learning from me—now our conversations are the easy chatter of old friends who have lots to share with one another. In fact, she was in my office recently, and before we knew it, two hours were gone! After we met, she fell in love with Blake, who is now her sweet husband. Before, we were the young and the old; now, we're the newlywed and the oldlywed. We are able to connect at a level of respect that says, "You matter, and I want to know what you think." We're friends. We love each other. We are almost fifty years apart, but we learn from each other with joy! We both need one another to fill out the gaps of "knowing" we have in our lives.

Cross-generational relationships are so important, but there are times when someone from our own generational tribe offers the best understanding. We can't miss the value of going through a season with others who dealt with the same thing and have perspective to offer—or even those who have only recently weathered the storm. Look at the popularity of mom groups and mom blogs. It's all in the connection that comes from sharing similar experiences. Having lived the same years with the same people gives a needed comfort zone. It's the same with AARP: Originally founded as a resource for people who are retired, the organization now appeals to millions of people, starting at age fifty. Why? Because life after fifty is an experience to be shared.

That being said, life pans out differently for every one of us. The next season, whether of our advancing age or otherwise, is unknown to us. We can take some courage from those who have already walked through it, but we also need our God.

God Is the God of Our Seasons

Sometimes recognizing God's role in our seasons can be hard. You may even feel as if He doesn't know what season you're in. You may feel as if He is somewhere "out there" but not close enough to hear your tremulous heart beating. You may feel as if you're on your own—but I can assure you that you are not.

God seems like a mysterious factor in our lives if we haven't gotten to know Him. It's hard to trust who or what we don't know, and that really seems to matter when it comes to the seasons that are out in front of us. Either we really know Him or we don't. If we know Him, we know He is in control of all things. If we believe He's in control, we can relax and know that He has placed us on this earth for His timing and His purposes. God is in control of every one of our seasons that ever was or ever shall be. He determined when we were born, and He already has determined our last day on earth. He is in complete charge and sovereignly rules over the depths and breadths of our lives. There is nothing He doesn't know about you or me, and His plans for us are good. Look at His words to us.

You have probably seen these verses many times, but read them anew in light of our "seasons."

> O LORD, You have searched me and known *me*.
> You know when I sit down and when I rise up;
> You understand my thought from afar.
> You scrutinize my path and my lying down,
> And are intimately acquainted with all my ways.
> Even before there is a word on my tongue,
> Behold, O LORD, You know it all. . . .
>
> I will give thanks to You, for I am fearfully
>   and wonderfully made;
> Wonderful are Your works,
> And my soul knows it very well.
> My frame was not hidden from You,
> When I was made in secret,
> *And* skillfully wrought in the depths of the earth;
> Your eyes have seen my unformed substance;
> And in Your book were all written
> The days that were ordained *for me*,
> When as yet there was not one of them.
>
> PSALM 139:1-4, 14-16

I love the fact that God has ordained our days and that His purposes for us in our seasons will never be thwarted. Proverbs 16:9 declares, "The mind of man plans his way, but the LORD directs his steps." Even if your season seems discouraging right now, you can be assured that the Lord is directing your steps, and He will continue to do so. He leaves it up to you to determine if you will trust Him with your days. It's when you try to dictate your seasons—how long they should last and what you expect of them—that you run into deep disappointment. I've learned that there is a God, and you and I are not Him.

Do you know that yet? That's a big "knowing" for us all. Everyone has to come to grips with it sooner or later—even kings who believe all power is theirs.

Consider the story of King Nebuchadnezzar: He thought he was bigger than God and said so. The Scriptures say that while his words were still in his mouth, "he was driven away from mankind and began eating grass like cattle, and his body was drenched with the dew of heaven until his hair had grown like eagles' feathers and his nails like birds' claws" (Daniel 4:33). After seven years of this humiliation, he said, "I, Nebuchadnezzar, raised my eyes toward heaven and my reason returned to me, and I blessed the Most High and praised and honored Him who lives forever" (verse 34). He was quick to declare to all,

All the inhabitants of the earth are accounted
　　as nothing,
But He does according to His will in the host
　　of heaven

And among the inhabitants of earth;
And no one can ward off His hand
Or say to Him, "What have you done?"

DANIEL 4:35

King Nebuchadnezzar became gloriously convinced that despite his own greatness, God was bigger and even more in control than he ever thought!

The prophet Jeremiah professed, "I know, O LORD, that a man's way is not in himself, nor is it in a man who walks to direct his steps" (Jeremiah 10:23). We are on life's moving sidewalk, and it is God who determines where it goes, how fast it moves, and when it stops. It's just that simple.

Elisabeth Elliot lived a full life on this earth. She had seasons of joy and seasons of great pain, such as when her first husband, Jim Elliot, was murdered by members of the Waodani tribe in South America. After his death, she and their young daughter, Valerie, returned to the village where they had served and courageously lived for five years with these same tribal people. Later, as a speaker and a writer, she inspired generations of women with her no-nonsense, "do the next thing and trust God" philosophy. Although she experienced the loss of another husband and had her own years of suffering with Alzheimer's disease before she died, she maintained her unwavering confidence in the God who had every season of her life in His control.

While she could still communicate, she frequently said, "Everything that happens to you has come through the hedge of His love."[4] I love the power behind those words. If we are called to endure anything of similar proportions, we, too, can know that God loves us and desires only good things for us. It may not always look "good" to us, but God's terms and definitions are often wildly different from ours—and so much better in the end.

My dear friend Kay Arthur has lived over eighty-three years and is still very active in ministry. In the seasons of her life, she has known the pain of an ex-husband's suicide; a son's estrangement; the death of a daughter-in-law; the trauma of another son's devastating, paralyzing disease; and the death of her beloved second husband, Jack, after fifty-one years of marriage. Like Elisabeth, Kay believes that "everything that comes into our lives is filtered through His fingers of love."[5] These two women confirm a truth we can claim for all times and seasons in our lives. Like many saints of old, they believe and rest in the sweet sovereignty and deep love of God. He knows our seasons and knows what He wants to accomplish with each of us on this earth.

God's love is unfathomable, and although His actions are often unexplainable, He never denies His great love for us, which is not a one-way street—loving God is a huge component in living well through our seasons. He is full of grace and knows the frailty of our bodies as we age. He's looking for those who will draw close to Him and love Him. The Scriptures tell us, "We love, because He first loved us" (1 John 4:19). So while our love for Him is a response to His love, we can't pout our way through life and call that "loving God." Loving Him is trusting Him; loving Him enables us to live our days relaxing in the truth that "underneath are the everlasting arms" (Deuteronomy 33:27).

We have yet to see what God has waiting for us once our time on this earth is completed. The seasons of our lives are both good and challenging, but while we try to cling to this life in every season, what is waiting is far better. Sometimes the seasons feel like a sleepless night, miserable and unending, but even so, the good news is that morning really will come. No season will last forever. Heaven waits, and we will live eternally there.

Just as it is written,

Things which eye has not seen and ear has not heard,
And which have not entered the heart of man,
All that God has prepared for those who love Him.

I CORINTHIANS 2:9

My hope is that this book will be a collection of life truths and navigational guides to help you along the way when you need it most. We all face unknown seasons, but you can take courage: God is the God of all our seasons. Nothing we face takes Him by surprise. He has already been there, and He's given us people, here and already gone, whose stories will encourage our hearts. It's always good to know others have made it through—and so can we!

No matter what season you are in, there are truths that can help you approach the unknown with confidence and hope. I've lived a lot of years, and my heart's desire is to share what I've learned as well as what others have shared about their journeys. Some things I've included are about our mentality in every unknown season: How can we be resilient? How can we overcome fear? And some things are going to walk you through how to face the specific unknown seasons ahead: seasons with adult children or aging parents, seasons with health struggles and grief. In all these, I want to be a guide walking beside you. I've been through these seasons, and I know you can face them with courage. Trust that God is the God of your season, no matter what it looks like, no matter how unknown.

CHAPTER TWO

RESILIENCE

---cපඩ්ර---

Resilience is accepting your new reality, even if it's less good
than the one you had before. You can fight it, you can do
nothing but scream about what you've lost, or you can accept
that and try to put together something that's good.

ELIZABETH EDWARDS

THE ABILITY TO BOUNCE BACK in the midst of adversity is a gift. The tenacity to make yourself get up and go again when you've been knocked down is a choice. The willingness to face a challenge even if you have no idea how you're going to overcome it is rooted in the belief that somehow God will provide what you need. We all admire people who are tenacious overcomers, and we sometimes wonder if we could react the same way in their circumstances.

We recognize this quality when we see it. We may not be able to put our finger on exactly what it is, but we know that it makes a difference not only in the life of the person who has it but also in the lives of those around her.

We are attracted to it. We want to hear about it. We want it for ourselves.

No one can begin to know how significant it is—until it's absent. A lack of it leads to problem upon problem and sorrow upon sorrow.

Some people have a natural bent toward it. Some people find it hard. But no matter—it can be learned. It can be embraced.

It's the one quality that gives living another day its hope.

It's called *resilience*.

My friend Nina is one of the most resilient women I know. She was a missionary to Eastern Europe for many years. Her health was compromised after she underwent radiation for pelvic cancer when she was a young woman. She has had twenty-eight surgeries since that time. One of the latest was a failed attempt to get her walking again. She has struggled for the last several years to gain the strength she needs to use her legs—nerve damage in her back has rendered her unable to walk. She has had to make the decision to move into an assisted-living facility; her room there, in size, is little more than a glorified closet. She has had to give up beautiful mementos collected overseas and precious personal effects.

When faced with a choice she didn't want to make, she said, in her typical inimitable way, "I am moving on to the next mission field! I look forward to what God has for me there!" She's always looking forward to the new day and always thanking God for His goodness all her years. She's seventy-three years old, confined to a wheelchair, single, and dependent on the kindness of friends to sustain her earthly existence. Yet she has a song in her heart, a smile on her face, and a forward-looking attitude that is totally contagious! She is resilient.

When changes come, resilience is what keeps us going forward. According to the American Psychological Association, "Resilience is the process of adapting well in the face of adversity, trauma, tragedy, threats, or significant sources of stress—such as family and relationship problems, serious health problems, or workplace and financial stressors."[1] It's not a call to "get over" something but rather an encouragement to be as strong as possible in the midst of it!

The opposite of resilience is not weakness but "learned helplessness." In his book *What Happy People Know,* Dan Baker says, "Learned helplessness can overtake almost anyone, but it most often occurs in three basic situations: when someone fails too many times; when someone is boxed in by a double-bind, lose-lose situation; or when someone is dominated by somebody else who takes away his opportunity to choose."[2] In other words, if you've tried and failed what feels like one too many times, if you are facing something with insurmountable odds, or if there is someone in your life who takes away your choice, then it would be easy for you to fall into learned helplessness. You give up because you just don't see any other way.

When unwanted changes come along, it's hard to think beyond the moment—beyond the fact that you are facing something you really don't want to face. But there are really just two choices: You either can sink into learned helplessness, or you can look your situation in the eye and decide to deal with it head-on! None of that means you don't hate the circumstances and wish they were different, but you are making a choice in your life. Believing you have the power to make a choice is the core of being resilient.

Nina has learned that she has colon cancer. Once again, she's faced with a choice: She can give in to despair and give up, or she can choose joy. She is consistently, joyfully thankful for how God has sustained her and given her faithful friends who are there for her. One lovely couple decorated her room with a new bed cover and window treatments. Nina publicly let others know how grateful she was.

When she later had to move to a new nursing facility, she uttered not a word of complaint. No lovely bed cover and window treatments there, but she keeps her trouble to herself and broadcasts her gratitude loudly. She finds her delight now in a bird feeder outside her window. How small her world has become! But there is no way that

Nina will allow learned helplessness to take her down. She knows the peril of her situation, but she is not going to allow it to overwhelm her. She recognizes the great power she has to choose and the great God who is with her every step of the way.

The unknown seasons can weigh us down because we can be tempted to borrow tomorrow's trouble. Nina has no idea what is waiting, but she knows that she's not heading toward a healthier future. The sense of hopelessness that goes along with that kind of story can be tough to deal with. If not combated with determination, it can lead into learned helplessness, which is a road to despondency and depression.

Learned helplessness is most likely to show up when we've experienced failure when it was important to succeed, rejection when we wanted to be accepted, and self-doubt when confidence would have been the winning ticket! These areas make a lot of sense when you think of the unknown seasons we all face. It is easy to succumb to despondency when we face repeated failures. Repeated rejections during a job search or repeated betrayals in a relationship can become weighty matters to a hurting heart. Self-doubt can move in like storm clouds, and thoughts of permanent failure can easily find a place to camp out. Do you know the feeling? If you do, you're not alone. Just about everyone who has lived and done anything has a failure story to tell. I know I do. Do you? Failure stories are part of all our lives, if we live long enough, and there's an odd sort of comfort when we're not the only ones who have failed.

I'm sitting here writing under the glow of a light bulb. The invention of the light bulb was the culmination of thousands of experiments that didn't work. Referencing this series of apparent failures, Thomas Alva Edison is reported to have said, "I have not failed 10,000 times. I have not failed once. I have succeeded in proving that those 10,000 ways will not work. When I have eliminated the ways that will not work, I will find the way that will work."[3] Edison kept on going, not letting failure take him down. Because he was resilient, today we have the light bulb and many other inventions that we take for granted.

If you've ever failed at something, you know how hard it is to try again. Just like the old adage says, "If you ever fall off a horse, the best cure is to get back on." Even if you are scared, climbing back in the saddle says, "I'm not defeated. I can do this." Some situations, however, lead to a greater struggle. When you reach the point where you know you can't do it, scared or any other way, resilience calls you to keep going.

Many of us remember Christopher Reeve, who played Superman in movies from the 1970s and '80s. He was handsome, strong, and seemingly indestructible. But then the day came when he was thrown from his horse and his spinal cord was crushed. He immediately became a quadriplegic. Superman was down—not out, but down. He was critically injured, and life as he knew it would never be the same. But he was a man of resilience.

Several years after the accident, he said, "You know, the accident's power is diminishing. Do I wish it hadn't happened? . . . Absolutely . . . but I find that it's best to think, well, what can I do today? Is there something I can accomplish, a phone call I can make, a letter I can write, a person I can talk to, that will move things forward? We have to learn to live a new life that would not have seemed possible. But that's not something you need to be Superman to accomplish."[4]

Acknowledging the reality of your situation is critical, but that reality doesn't have to stop you from going forward. Christopher Reeve didn't allow his injury to stop him. While he couldn't just get back on the horse as a way of coping, he traveled on behalf of people with spinal cord injuries and stayed on the task until the day he breathed his last labored breath.

I'm convinced that whatever your losses or failures, true resilience comes with the determination to go with what you've got left. It's not what you've lost but what remains that matters. It doesn't mean you won't long for what you had, especially if your life has been permanently altered. No need to be unrealistic about that.

Ellie is a sweet young woman who was driving home on a very hot day with the window down in her car because her air-conditioning was broken. She had just left her babysitting job. A man swerved into her lane, and when she swerved to miss him, she lost control of her car. It skidded off the road and rolled on its side, severing her left arm in the process. A man saw the crash and immediately jumped out of his car to see if he could help. Although at first he thought she was gone, he heard a slight moan and quickly pulled off his business shirt to make a tourniquet. Things did not look good, but he knew he had to try to save this college student with her whole life ahead of her. He saved her from bleeding out, and Ellie was soon transported to the hospital.

Her arm could not be saved. At age nineteen, her whole world changed forever. She would face a future with what she had left. She needed to make a choice: Give up or go on. Yes, she has battled sadness, feelings of helplessness, and phantom pains in an arm that is no longer there. She will always be minus the arm that gave her balance, ability, and skill. That is an unchangeable fact.

However, another fact is that she also has traveled to Africa and China on behalf of Joni and Friends to minister to people with disabilities. She traveled alone, with interruptions and complications that would frustrate the most seasoned, able-bodied traveler, but she did it. Today she is married to a man who loves her with an unconditional love. She struggles with what she can't do and laments the loss of her arm, but she sees God's goodness in it all to give her the love of her life. She goes on, forever changed, but embracing what she has left as a good, good gift.

Resilience Is Not Just Wishful Thinking

Resilience is not wishful thinking, positive thinking, or denial. It is the ability to optimistically view the future, even when the worst has happened. It is the capacity to recognize the truth and accept it, to look at the future with hope and realism, and to accept God's dealings with you as good. When hard things happen, God doesn't turn His back. In fact, I believe He leans in closer and reminds us in a thousand ways that He is good all the time.

Even in His goodness, however, He doesn't necessarily change our circumstances. We still go through brutal, wintry seasons when others around us are enjoying spring. But resilience allows us to continue with dignity and purpose. Anything else really is learned helplessness.

Notice that the phrase *learned helplessness* is all about what is learned. It is not natural to humans to be helpless, but life experiences can stamp helplessness on our brains. Such an imprint gives a sense of impossibility to a situation. Psychologist Martin Seligman has discovered that people do best when they look forward to what *can be* rather than looking backward to *what was*.[5] I love his approach because I've seen how freeing it is in my own life. I don't like dwelling on losses and hard times, so I've learned to look forward to places where there are gains and good times. Granted, there are tough things to face in life, but we don't have to dwell in the awfulness of our situation. If we do, then learned helplessness is what awaits. It is the place we can go to let ourselves off the hook rather than trying again. It's the room where the walls are painted with hopelessness and where we can rehearse our losses and pain. It feels right when we begin to pour out our woes, but if we begin to feel too at home there, we find we are drained of the energy we need to live.

My friend Dr. Helen McIntosh certainly could have chosen to resort to the sad, hopeless room of learned helplessness. She has every reason to dwell there. She doesn't have any good outcomes to look forward to. She is a young seventy-three-year-old who was diagnosed with Parkinson's disease several years ago. This disease doesn't offer hope for getting better with an improved lifestyle. The only future it offers is less mobility and physical stress. Helen was fully aware of this when she was diagnosed. She had seen others go through the downhill slide to total incapacitation. Talk about a state of helplessness! But Helen made a choice—to make the most of what was a powerful inevitability in her life.

She is a professional psychologist who has worked with adults and children for years, helping them to see a better way. She is a wife, mother, grandmother, and professional who happens to have an incurable disease. She is beautiful, clever, and full of love. One day when we were talking about life, I asked her to give me an insight into her resilient spirit, which never seems to flag or fail. In her typical "in the moment" way, she answered my question by referencing a note someone else with Parkinson's had sent her:

Today someone sent me a saying by Vivian Greene: "Life isn't about waiting for the storm to pass . . . It's about learning to dance in the rain!" I think that's resilience. It's choosing life *anyway*. It's making the choice to move forward *anyway*. A sentence I have said to myself for decades is "I choose to be okay no matter what." It's from a deep knowing inside of me that circumstances can rule anyone's life, but I can choose that they *not* rule mine. They cannot rule me or my emotions. At the same time, I desperately want to be honest with myself and others about the pain, difficulties, and discomfort in the journey. I don't want to pretend that there are no obstacles—even though I still step out on the floor and dance! I have found "resilience" to be the freest place of all. It keeps me from breaking down in this journey. I could have gotten stuck on this Parkinson's road I'm traveling, but I haven't. I am moving *anyway*![6]

Candidly, everything Helen does is hard. Getting dressed, rising from a chair, eating a meal, smiling, keeping her eyelids open—the list goes on and on. She could just declare, "I can't; it's too hard!" and quickly become an invalid. Instead, she has chosen to do it *anyway*! Even if it's hard, takes twice as much time to do what others do quickly, or zaps her of energy, she is determined to do it *anyway*.

This is where the voice of the pessimist can easily take over the conversation. "And what is the value of that kind of effort? You're not going to win this battle anyway."

That voice, if allowed to speak, will whine you into a place of despair, which is always a place of decline. We all have that kind of voice living in our brains. We can summon the pessimist to the microphone at any given moment. It starts with "I can't" and moves to "What's the use?" and ends up in the pit of despair. Pessimism can take you to rooms with no exits in a house of learned helplessness. That is why recognizing and quieting it before it has time to speak is one of the most critical steps you can take to overcoming learned helplessness.

My friend Jenny Suddeth could so easily have let herself live there. She is a young woman no one would blame for giving up and sinking into self-pity and the accompanying helplessness. When she thinks of her life, it would be so simple just to say, "Why fight it?" She's had a brain tumor once and breast cancer twice. Her young daughters were involved in a serious bus wreck. And she says, "That was easy compared to the emotional pain that has come with

being a pastor's wife for twenty-five years." There is so
much buried between the layers of those words. Can you
hear it? The saving grace of her difficult life experience is
that she has learned to look away from her own situation
and look at others:

> When I look around, I am overwhelmed with the
> strength others show, and it encourages me. I can
> then be resilient. I can bounce back. I can keep
> going. I can be thankful. It becomes a choice.
> And it is good. So much is good. Besides, have I
> forgotten? God is good! He has my very best in
> mind. Resilience means that even when hard things
> have been tossed my way, I can choose to do the
> next right thing by taking the next step, saying the
> next kind word, serving the next person, and taking
> the next look at what I have been given, more than
> staring at what has been taken away. There is always
> something to be thankful for.[7]

Do You Want to Choose Resilience?
Maybe you are facing a change in your life that seems
insurmountable. Maybe it's a diagnosis that has blindsided
you or a relationship that has taken a hard turn, or maybe
you have lost someone with whom you planned to grow
old. Perhaps death has brought a change in your life and
suddenly you are in the season of having been left behind.

What is the message you speak to yourself? What are the words that only you hear?

Listen to what you are saying to yourself about your situation. Take a giant step back and assess what you are saying to you. It's critical to your capacity to be resilient.

Remind yourself that you're not the first.
There is nothing new under the sun, including your affliction, failure, or loss. That doesn't make your pain go away, but it will affect how you handle your pain. There is something comforting in knowing that others have hurt in the same way, others have walked through the same valley, others have borne the same grief.

There is a fellowship of suffering among those who go through similar struggles. It seems to me that spring and winter bring the most difficult struggles. One speaks of new beginnings, tender young ones, and fragile flowers. I see so many young people in the season of spring who have made big plans—and yet their plans fall down around them. Often the sources of their self-doubt and fear are love that disappoints or love that never comes. *Am I not good enough? Am I a bad person? Why doesn't someone come along and love me?* In these times, when *commitment* is a hard word for so many to wrap their heads around, young people are left with a fear of permanence and yet are anxious that all relationships may really be temporary. While they long for the constancy of marriage, they are fearful of the longevity of marriage. They fear drawing close because they could be hurt or left. Some make it over the finish line and through the ceremony, only to find in a couple of years that they have no idea who their mate is. Some never make it. At best the adjustments can be daunting. No matter what the emotional angst is, spring can be a tough time to be resilient.

In my spring season, I remember crying to no one in particular that my heart was broken. I felt I'd probably never get over it. I dated a guy in college who had a smooth, romantic way about him. When I transferred to another college, he promised to be true. I believed him and plotted out a future with him that I thought would be sweet. You can only imagine my shock when, within the year, he married my former roommate.

Hindsight is a glorious thing. I'm so glad we didn't marry, and I imagine he is as well. I've lost track of him and my old roommate, but I pray that they have had a good, long, happy married life. I know that the man I met later was a wonderful gift from God. We've been married fifty years, and I wouldn't have wanted to do life with anyone else.

Spring can be tough, but winter can be a hard season too. Winter is going to come no matter what we do. We can't hold it back. So we can either prepare for it by preparing our minds as much as possible, which will produce resilience, or we can let it just overtake us and weaken us.

As Madame de Staël once said, "When a noble life has prepared for old age, it is not decline that it reveals, but the first days of immortality."

Resilience in the winter days is the choice to keep your soul engaged with life and the Lord of life. I love this quote by George Sand: "Try to keep your soul young and quivering right up to old age." We all will do it differently, but keeping our thoughts as young and alive as possible is a choice we must pursue as God gives us grace. If He's been there in the past, He'll be there in the days when the chill of winter moves in:

> The godly will flourish like palm trees
>   and grow strong like the cedars of Lebanon.
> For they are transplanted to the LORD's own house.
>   They flourish in the courts of our God.
> Even in old age they will still produce fruit;
>   they will remain vital and green.
> They will declare, "The LORD is just!
>   He is my rock!
>   There is no evil in him!"

PSALM 92:12-15, NLT

Refrain from falling into the pit of comparison.
Life is not fair, and when it goes against you, it's better to ask "Why not?" rather than "Why me?" The people who ask "Why me?" have already lost their foothold on resil-

ience. We all can look around and see those who have fared much worse than we have and those who have fared much better. Resting in the sweet, sovereign will of God is one of the most relaxing places to be. Because He deals with each of us differently, and because His purposes for each of us are different, comparing our life circumstances with another human being's is folly.

When we fall into comparison's trap, we've forgotten that the last chapter of our lives hasn't yet been written! As long as there is life and breath, God is writing more chapters. What seems like an unfair deal now may well be the stepping-stone to something great we never knew.

Don't underestimate the power of support.

Going through unknown seasons can be better when you have support. If someone has been there or is there, exploring what he or she might have to say can be helpful. If you aren't encouraged, though, then don't hang around. You can decide what you do and don't do. If you encounter a group of victims who have only found their common denominator in learned helplessness, run and don't look back. If you find a group of gnarly survivors who simply will not throw in the towel, then hang around them and soak up some of their optimism. They will be good for you. They will be support.

When seasons change and you are confronted with health issues or relationship issues or loss that you can't bear, the worst thing to do is to withdraw. True friends who have known you in the good days will be your best allies in the tough days. They will stay with you through it all. I've found that most friends want to remain friends through thick and thin, but too often the person going through the hard season withdraws. It is hard to be a friend to someone who isolates, and yet being a friend and having a friend at that time are the most important things any of us can do.

My dear, dear friend Charlotte left this earth at a very young sixty-eight years old. Her life was fraught with incredible pain and loss. She was diagnosed with cancer, her husband was diagnosed with multiple sclerosis, and two of her four children died tragically. For many years, she withdrew and didn't seem to want to be with old friends. Near the end of her life, however, when it was clear the cancer could not be defeated, I think she remembered the close, loving path we had walked before. Now it was time to walk that path together again until the end. So she asked to meet for weekly lunches with her girlfriends. We did this as long as she was able. Then when her last days came and she was confined to bed, she still wanted to have time together. She gave us her books and costume jewelry—tender reminders that our friendship had been life-giving to each of us. She left this world knowing that her friends were with her and had walked her to the very gates of heaven. It was a tender reminder that friends are rich sources of support who need to be cherished and remembered.

Move toward God instead of away from Him.

The more strenuous the season, the more your years of knowing God will manifest their value. Some people move away from God, thinking He's abandoned them when their seasons grow cold. That reaction strips us of our comfort and takes away every bit of our resilience. Any bitterness or doubt that creeps into our hearts will weaken resilience. Our ability to bounce back and stay strong is weakened exponentially when we succumb to doubts and bitterness about God and His goodness. The reality is that He never abandons us; it is we who walk away from Him.

That's the reason it's important to spend time soaking our minds in the Scriptures and listening to songs that speak the great truths of the faith. If the Scriptures are in us, they will come back to us. When we are still, they will come to the forefront of our minds. You may ask, "What if they are not in me? What do I do?" Well, there's good news: Listening to Scripture on CD or MP3 will fill your mind with the power and riches of the Word. I love *The Word of Promise Audio Bible* I have on my phone. Anytime I need to bathe my mind with the ancient wisdom of the Scriptures, that's where I go. I also can access music that has inspired me in years past and new songs that grab my heart now. In listening and allowing my mind to be bathed in the wonders of God's Word and the songs of the faith, I am making my mind and emotions fertile fields for the joy and freedom of resilience.

One of my favorite resilience-producing Scriptures is Psalm 27:13-14:

> I would have despaired unless I had believed that
>> I would see the goodness of the LORD
> In the land of the living.
> Wait for the LORD;
> Be strong and let your heart take courage;
> Yes, wait for the LORD.

Joseph Benson's commentary on this passage says it so well: "Keep up thy spirits in the midst of thy greatest dangers and difficulties: let thy heart be fixed, trusting in God, and thy mind stayed on him, and then none of these things will move thee."[8]

That's the point! That "none of these things" will move us. That is the core of resilience, no matter the season in which you find yourself.

CHAPTER THREE

FIGHT FEAR

Without fear, there cannot be courage.

ERAGON

WHEN YOU ARE IN AN UNKNOWN SEASON, fear is like a creepy, unwanted neighbor who lurks around, holding signs of doom. He changes the signs from time to time just so you'll let your guard down, but every time you look up, he's there with his terrifying threats:

"You aren't the person you used to be."

"You are becoming invisible."

"You are losing your beauty."

"You're going to get cancer."

"You're going to be alone."

"Your pain will be unbearable."

"Your children don't want to be with you."

"Your mate is going to die."

"You are going to get Alzheimer's."

"You have made such a mess of your life; you'll never be able to recover."

"You are irrelevant."

"You can't afford to live."

"You're going to die, and it's going to be awful."

Fear feels like such a dark, demeaning presence in our lives, but it's really in our lives for a good purpose. Despite its tendency to get out of control, fear is part of a wonderful system that was designed to help us survive. It's the trigger for the fight-or-flight mechanism God graciously put in our brains to cause us to react appropriately when faced with danger. The problem is that fear has to be managed or it will run rampant, creating all kinds of anxiety, depression, hostility, and sadness.

In many of us, fear seems to be on high alert. It doesn't have to be faced with a real situation to go to work. All it needs is a suggestion, a hint, or a rumor before it starts pulling all the levers and pushing all the knobs, releasing the cascade of hormones that causes us to be scared to death! Our thinking is what controls it, and if we buy into the suggestions and stories around us, we're going to see the worst of it.

Our ability to manage fear is the number one factor in determining how well we will navigate the unknown seasons of our lives. We may fear something as simple as an awkward social situation or something as horrible as being raped and murdered. Fear doesn't need a real situation; all it needs is a thought. Understanding how fear affects us is critical to our ability to cope with the feelings that seem to crop up uninvited during every season of our lives. This is especially true during the winter season when things can become so bleak.

Take a minute to think about your top three fears. Don't try to be rational about them—just jot them down quickly in the next thirty seconds:

1.

2.

3.

I found this little exercise to be quite revealing. Here are my fears as they stand today:

1. *Closed places.* I don't like elevators, MRIs, or the window seat on airplanes. I will subject myself to all three if I have to, but I don't enjoy them!

2. *Riding with people whose driving I don't trust.* I do submit myself to these situations, but I don't like them and am not comfortable. I'd rather drive myself.

3. *Being alone in my old age.* I think this fear has to do with friends not being there. I've lost several very good friends to death in the past couple of years, and I'm wondering who's going to be left.

As I look at my top three fears, I see some of my need to control rearing its ugly head. I think fear likes to capitalize on things we can't control. Anything that feels "beyond my control" creates a panic response.

When a friend goes through a traumatic experience, do you ever catch yourself thinking, *I don't know how she deals with that?* The thought behind that may really be, *I don't think I could bear to go through what she's going through.* In other words, you have concluded that there are things in life that are unbearable. Your fight-or-flight mechanism stays on high alert when you think or hear about such an occurrence. One of fear's most convincing lies is *You will not be able to stand living through such an occurrence.* Yet somehow other people manage to live through it. You may not want to live through these things, but you can! Life doesn't allow us to choose our circumstances or our pain.

I have a dear older friend I have known since I was twelve years old. She is now ninety-eight and living in an assisted-living facility. She has survived car accidents, back surgeries, strokes, falls, total hearing loss, and near-blindness. She wonders why the Lord has kept her here so long, and yet she lives. When I look at her situation, my first thought is always this: *I don't think I could stand to live like that.* Of course, the reality is that I could if I had to, though I really don't want to. We all could do it. We all may die in our sleep, but should we have to live an extended period in a debilitating situation, we have my friend's example and the stories of so many others. Their "winter seasons" have been long and arduous, and yet they find the grace to keep on living until the date that God has marked on His calendar for them to die.

In contrast, my beloved pastor and dear friend Wayne Barber died as I was writing this book. He was ill for a short time with an undiagnosed disease. Despite seeing many doctors and enduring a spinal surgery recommended to correct his symptoms, he never got better. Then, to the surprise of everyone, he died in his sleep. He had just turned seventy-three. He was young in today's reckoning of age and was still an active pastor in a flourishing church. Yet clearly his expiration date was August 29, 2016, because that's the day he went to be with the Lord. In this, too, I must trust that God knows. And since I trust Him, I have to leave it with Him. Oh, how I hate it—but it is either trust or sink into an inconsolable grief.

How do I know that God is so specific that He has already appointed the days of our birth and death? Well, as I study Scripture, I don't find much that He leaves to chance. He is sovereign over all things. Here is just one of the places where God shows us this:

Your eyes have seen my unformed substance;
And in Your book were all written
The days that were ordained *for me*,
When as yet there was not one of them.

PSALM 139:16

I know there are many questions about God's sovereignty, but here's the truth: If He's not sovereign over everything, then things slip through the cracks. If He lets things slip through the cracks, then how can we trust Him with our lives and the lives of those we love? To believe that God is sovereign over every season is to believe that nothing is out of His sight or His care. It is to be convinced that He's not just a "little bit sovereign," to quote Chuck Swindoll,[1] but that He's totally sovereign, no matter how out of control things feel.

My grandmother lived to be thirty-six years old. Yes, you read that right. She was thirty-six when she gave birth to her tenth child and died three weeks later. Did she slip through the cracks, or did God have a plan in allowing her to live that short period of time? I have to believe He was in charge even in that season when she had everything to live for and was desperately needed in her home. How on earth could a sovereign God allow such a thing? And yet if He didn't allow it, then fate or luck was in charge, and there was absolutely no purpose in this pain to her and her family. Was it just bad luck that she was born before penicillin was discovered? Was it just fate that her tenth childbirth went wrong? I would rather believe that she was in the hands of an all-sovereign God who loved her well.

Apologist Ravi Zacharias says,

> When God is our Holy Father, sovereignty, holiness, omniscience, and immutability do not terrify us; they leave us full of awe and gratitude. Sovereignty is only tyrannical if it is unbounded by goodness; holiness is only terrifying if it is untempered by grace; omniscience is only taunting if it is unaccompanied by mercy; and immutability is only torturous if there is no guarantee of goodwill.[2]

Our fundamental belief in the sovereignty and love of God is the only antidote we have for the fears of this world. Many of us struggle with the need to control, and knowing what we can't control engenders fear. The reality is that there are so many things out of our control. What can we really control? Can we hold back the winds of a tornado? Can we keep another driver from hitting us head-on? Can we protect our children from a predator in the family? Can we make our children love God? Can we make our mate stay faithful? Can we prevent terrorist attacks? Can we keep disease and the ravages of old age from knocking on our doors? The list could go on and on. Whatever the human mind can conceive can test our capacity to control.

When we encounter things in the natural world and in the diabolical mind of man that are bigger than we are, we have no control. We can either bow to God's sovereignty and unconditional love or we can become fear-torn victims in an out-of-control world.

So what do we do about fear?

Recognize that everyone is afraid of something, though we may not all be afraid of the same things. For instance, spiders don't bother me at all. I figure I can get rid of the bad ones and leave the good ones alone. I have no visceral response when I see a spider. I have a son, however, who has never met a spider he could tolerate. Spiders tap into some kind of fear in him, which is a nice way of saying they give him the creeps.

Sometimes the unknown season we are entering creates irrational fears that run out ahead of us. When we are in our young child-raising years, we may hear that having teenagers is an impossible season—but people live through it somehow. And most of us look back with fondness on those crazy-making years that allowed our children to become adults.

Who hasn't been warned about menopause and all its physical manifestations? Everyone is different. For some, "going through the change" is a trying season, and for others, not so much. Regardless, somehow we live.

Who hasn't been told that "old age isn't for sissies"? And yet all of us have known amazing seniors who have proven themselves to be heroes. They've called back to us and said, "It's not so bad. It's good to be old. Consider the alternative."

There's enough truth in all those scenarios to at least put us on guard. But who is to say that we are going to have the same experiences as those who have struggled and suffered? To believe what you hear and think that it will be your experience is called "borrowing trouble." Fear loves when we do that because it gives free rein to scare us in so many colorful ways!

Fear and a Good Brain Don't Mix

Perhaps you've heard the words *catastrophizing* or *awfulizing*. If you have, you know that neither of them is good. If you haven't heard of these concepts before, look at their roots: *catastrophe* and *awful*—ugly words that mean nothing good. Yet many of us have been trained to see things through a lens that "awfulizes" whatever comes. When we think in these ways, we are setting our bodies up for a reaction that has no good results. Many of us don't pay attention to the way we think. We don't believe it has an effect or that it really matters when it comes to our physical well-being, but it does.

Fear can be helpful when we need to run or fight because we're in danger, but when we're just sitting still and ruminating over what could happen, it sets us up for a negative physical experience. Excessive worry and anxiety do nothing for us but cloud the way we see what's going on in our lives. How we view what happens determines how our bodies will respond. We need to ask, *Is the thing that's worrying me really awful? Is it really a catastrophe? Or is it my perception that is causing my body to release stress hormones such as cortisol and adrenaline?* Again, those things aren't bad—unless they're constant. When we live in a state of fear, a cascade of physical ills can follow.

Do you recognize any of these annoying physical manifestations of anxiety?

> Dizziness
> Dry mouth
> Fast heartbeat
> Headaches
> Stomachaches
> Irritability
> Muscle tension
> Inability to concentrate
> Nausea
> Shortness of breath
> Sweating

When we allow worry and anxiety to become chronic, the fight-or-flight reaction causes the body's sympathetic nervous system to release stress hormones, which can boost our sugar levels and blood fats (triglycerides). That's all good if you need fuel to escape a pursuing tiger, but if the "tiger" is worry and anxiety you can't outrun, then these stress hormones can do damage. They can suppress your immune system, affect your short-term memory, tighten your muscles, upset your stomach, give you premature coronary artery disease, and even bring on a heart attack. Oh dear! All of that from your body's response to ugly fear.

How well we're able to cope with stress really determines whether our bodies will release unnecessary hormones. You remember the old axiom "It's not what happens to you but how you respond that matters"? It is so very true. How you respond to your situation has a big role in determining whether the stress in your life will make you sick or not. This is why it's critical to keep a check on attitudes. Pessimism that goes unchecked is fuel for fear. If you believe that nothing will ever get better and no good can come out of what you're experiencing, that attitude of defeat will do a number on your brain as you move through the changing seasons of your life.

Maybe you're saying to yourself, *Well, I'm out of luck, then, because I'm just pessimistic. It's hard for me to look at an unknown season and be anything but worried.* I understand. There are people who naturally lean toward pessimism, just as there are people who are just naturally optimistic. But that doesn't mean our brains can rule us. We have to tell them what to think. We have been given the capacity to override our brains with the truth, no matter what their natural bent might be. By deciding what we will think about, we can override our own tendency to get out of bounds with pessimism or optimism. Either inclination, when left on its own, can wreak havoc. Out-of-control pessimism can keep us from ever seeing the hope that is truly there; out-of-control optimism will keep us from seeing the warning signs to be careful. Either extreme will cost us. There is a lot to be said for the middle ground of truth. It defies pessimism and tempers optimism.

This is where brain care becomes essential to walking through the unknown seasons. It's so much better to get a head start on how we think before we hit challenging times of change. Let's face it: Fear is always about the future. We wonder how it will feel to go through whatever waits, and sometimes we drag our past experiences into the future, thinking that we can't possibly live through another experience like what we've already gone through. Ever felt like that?

When my daddy was dying, I remember walking around a grocery store, wondering how it would feel not to have a dad. I'd lived almost fifty years with a father, and now it seemed his body was preparing to leave the earth. I was worried about the future I would face without him. I made it through each painful day of his leaving, and when he breathed his last, I then knew how it felt not to have a dad. Yet I lived through it.

I still miss him, but I don't miss sitting by his bed, trying to reason with his combative dementia. I no longer have a fear of life without him, because I lived through that awful season of his dying. Now all I have are sweet memories: I can look back and remember what I want to. That's part of brain care. His exit was an awful time, but it was not the sum total of my life with him.

When it came time for my mother to leave, the whole experience was different. She was an invalid, confined to a bed due to a broken hip that didn't heal, but her mind was totally intact. She spoke with great clarity and understanding until the very end. When she was dying, I knew what it would be like to live without a parent. I knew I would survive her absence.

I miss her, but I'm not haunted by memories of things I should have done or said. I have no regrets even though I was not with her when she died. She was in a hospital in Alabama, and I was on a plane trying to get there from California. I could bring up my sad memories from that Monday when I was trying to get to her side. I could bring up memories of turning my phone on when the plane landed in Chattanooga and seeing the call that I knew meant she had died.

I was her only child, and I wasn't there. I could go back and visit those feelings of frustration from the past, but I won't and I don't. What good would it do? All the events from that day are available in my memories, but I have no intention of accessing them. I know they're there, but to revisit them is just to drag my emotions through pain I can do nothing about.

Taking Care of Your Brain

Brain care keeps us aware that our fears are about a future we don't know and that our past experiences are unique to a past we don't have to remember or repeat unless we choose to. Brain care is an awareness of what we can and cannot do with our brains. There are a few specific things we need to pay attention to in order to take good care of our brains.

Be wise with the past.

We have a limbic system in our brains that operates the autonomic nervous system. One of the things it does is to act as a trauma control center, regulating fear conditioning and memory storage. The specific parts of the limbic system that operate these processes are the amygdala and the hippocampus, two important parts of your brain. You can't erase what they have recorded—what is there is there.

The amygdala has a lot to do with our fears and phobias, and the hippocampus concerns itself with our emotional and long-term memory as well as our fears and anxieties. It assesses incoming information for its emotional significance, so trying to find peace by getting rid of past memories isn't possible. They are all stored in the amygdala.

Picking at pain has never been a good idea, and trying

to figure out how to make the hurt stop by dissecting it is counterproductive. It just keeps the memories raw. But even though it hurts, acknowledging pain is good. As long as you can own it and remember that other people have lived through it, you will find the courage to believe you can as well.

Be at peace with the future.
Looking at the future with dread will also cause your brain problems. Because we don't know the future, we can never make a perfect decision, so deciding to dread the days ahead is a bad choice. Whatever is out there cannot be stopped by our worry. The good news is that God lived in the past, lives in the present, and already lives in the future. That's one of the reasons His sovereignty is such a sweet place to abide. He's already lived the days ahead of us. His eternality gives Him a view we can never hope to have with all our imaginings. We might try to figure out how many years we have ahead of us, but the truth is that we can't know. So why worry about it? Jesus said, "Which of you by worrying can add a single hour to his life's span?" (Luke 12:25).

Be anxious for nothing.
So if worry and anxiety are so bad for our brains and bodies, what can we do about it? Well, God has given us the perfect formula in Scripture, although it really seems too simple to work. The apostle Paul writes in Philippians (a

book about how to have joy no matter what!), "Be anxious for nothing, but in everything by prayer and supplication with thanksgiving let your requests be made known to God. And the peace of God, which surpasses all comprehension, will guard your hearts and your minds in Christ Jesus" (4:6-7). Perhaps this thought is new to you, or perhaps you can quote these verses from memory, but it's critical to tap into the genius of what the Bible says here.

Look at it: Stop being anxious—not a suggestion but a command. Stop it! If that were all God wanted us to do, that would be enough, though surely it would feel cruel. But since He's a good God, He doesn't want us to simply "stop worrying." Instead, He gives us a perspective that totally corresponds to what is happening in our brains. After all, He is the Creator, the One who made that three pounds of tissue in your skull!

God wants us to stop being anxious about *anything*. There are no exceptions: tornadoes, cancer, ISIS, betrayal, floods, thieves, heart attacks, abusers, wild tigers— anything else you can think of. And how are we supposed to stop it? Paul writes, "In everything by prayer and supplication with thanksgiving let your requests be made known to God."

In other words, stop being anxious! Stop ruminating over the things you are worried about, no matter how horrendous they are. Talk to God about those things. Come to Him in prayer. That means directly addressing Him, not just thinking about Him or meditating on what He says in His Word or reading devotionals about Him. It's using His name and speaking to Him directly.

Prayer, very simply, is talking to God. "Be anxious for nothing, but in everything by prayer and supplication with thanksgiving" means "Talk to God. Quit talking to yourself and others about everything that is wrong or could happen or perhaps has happened. God is the One who can and will provide an answer for you."

Paul even specifically uses the word *supplication*, which means asking for what you want or need. He says, "Talk to God and tell Him what you need." God wants us to make an entreaty, and He takes it seriously, seeing beyond the desire we're presenting to Him.

Dr. Michael Williams gives an interesting insight into supplication, a word we don't often use:

> Supplication is commonly defined as (1): "The action of asking or begging for something earnestly or humbly." . . . The word supplication comes from a Latin term, supplicare, which means to plead humbly and has the word supple as its root. . . .
>
> When we pray with supplication, we are not only humbly submitting our requests to God, we're doing it with the mindset of allowing our minds to be supple and receptive to God's will. We want God to mold our thinking, our opinions,

and our emotions to be in line with His thinking, opinions, and emotions. When this happens, God changes us to be more like His Son, which changes our desires and our will to be in line with His.[3]

Anxiety, rooted in our fears, drives us away from God— unless we turn toward Him, willing to let Him work in our own hearts and do some molding while He's handling our anxious thoughts.

Prayer paired with supplication is an amazing process, but God doesn't stop with that. The next piece of our Philippians passage can give us spiritual whiplash. Right in the middle of our anxiety, we're told not only to talk to God and to spell out our requests with a supple heart in which He can work, but also to do it all with thanksgiving.

"Really, Lord?" you may ask. "I'm so worried and afraid and panicked over what might happen. Can You not just fix it and take away the problem?" Being thankful at this point seems way out of bounds. It can even feel unfair. But then God puts a final nail in anxiety's coffin—thanksgiving will open a glorious door to the peace you really want.

That seems so implausible, but look at this whole thought: The word for *thanksgiving* in the original Greek is *eukharistia,* which means to be full of thanks and praise. It's a simple but profound concept that changes everything: At the moment we begin being grateful, something changes in our brains. The Creator knows! Fear recedes, gratefulness comes forward, and peace overtakes.

In his wonderful book *What Happy People Know,* Dan Baker says,

> It is a fact of neurology that the brain cannot be in a state of appreciation and a state of fear at the same time. The two states may alternate, but are mutually exclusive. . . .
>
> When you enter into the active condition of appreciation . . . creativity flows, heart rate slows, brain waves soften into rolling ripples, and an exquisite calm descends over your entire being. During active appreciation, your brain, heart, and endocrine system work in synchrony and heal in harmony.[4]

What your stress reaction destroys, your response of gratitude can heal—"and the peace of God, which surpasses all comprehension, will guard your hearts and your minds in Christ Jesus" (Philippians 4:7).

God's formula works. I love that His peculiar peace surpasses understanding. It makes no sense, but it works. He created us that way. As St. Augustine so aptly said, "Thou hast made us for Thyself and our hearts are restless till they rest in Thee."[5] That rest does not come until we willingly submit to the fact that He is God, and we are not. We can talk with Him, telling Him our deepest hurts and greatest needs, all the while thanking Him for being God. What an interesting antithesis that is to the person who becomes angry with God in the midst of her fear, shaking her fist and deciding to take a stance of chronic hostility. I've heard people say, "God is big. He can handle my anger." And yes, He is big and unscathed by our anger—but He has given us the way to have peace in the midst of our anxiety: prayer, supplication, and thanksgiving. Nowhere do I read in Scripture, "Go ahead and be angry with Him. He can take it." Of course He can take it, but should He just sit back and let you beat on His all-loving chest, thinking you can angrily manipulate Him? No. Gratitude changes the whole picture.

As we close out this chapter, take some time to begin listing all the things for which you can thank God. Then keep adding to it as the days and weeks roll along. You'll be amazed at the peace that follows. The problems may not change, but you will. And as you do, you'll find your anxiety dissipating. It's a gift from your Father.

CHAPTER FOUR

DON'T FORGET TO LAUGH

———— ⬦ ————

Laughter is the finest sound there is. . . . It's the best thing about
us and it lasts until the game is called on account of darkness.

LINDA ELLERBEE, *Move On*

"E-T-H-I-C-S." My daddy spelled the word with great
precision as he told the young physical therapist massag-
ing his frozen shoulder that she needed to go away. She
laughingly asked him why as she continued to massage.
He explained very clearly that it was a matter of "ethics." The twentysomething therapist took the cue and
climbed down from her perch on the side of his hospital
bed. Daddy seemed very self-righteously pleased when she
stopped. My mother and I, who were sitting on a couch
and watching the whole scenario, began to giggle. Ethics?
Where had that word come from? He had been in a state

of dementia, confined to a hospital bed for several months, and it had been a long time since we'd had a lucid conversation with him. It had been a painful time—but when he came out with that comment, we both fell over in a heap! Laughing was good for our souls. It broke the tension of watching the deterioration of a man we both loved dearly.

The three of us were in a season none of us had asked for: my dad, confused and confined to a hospital bed in the living room of their home; my mother, taking care of him 24/7; me, their only child. We were a ragged troupe engulfed in the emotions this kind of season brings. That's why we had to laugh when Daddy came up with the spelling bee moment. E-T-H-I-C-S indeed!

Before the dementia set in, my dad was a funny man. He had a quick wit and a sense of timing that was impeccable. Any moment could take a humorous turn with him. I think that was another reason Mother and I had to giggle. For one brief moment, the sad scene became a bit lighter. We could laugh in the middle of it all. It was possible! And it felt good!

Laughter is a wonderful gift, something to be cherished and enjoyed no matter what season you are in. We often forget the importance of laughter, especially when we are going through a season of change and uncertainty. When death changes the dynamic, when illness steals the joy, when separation alters the security, when rebellion rips sweet love from your heart, sometimes the best thing you can do is laugh. Many times seasonal transitions take your breath away and leave you feeling as if you will never laugh again. Sometimes guilt sets in. There's a sense that if someone you love has died or is suffering deeply, it would be inappropriate or even disrespectful to laugh. To find something funny when your heart is breaking seems to work against all that seems right. Yet God designed laughter to bring a beautiful release.

I mentioned that my pastor and friend Wayne Barber died recently. At his Celebration of Life service, his son, Steven, who loved and appreciated his daddy's sense of humor, gave a bit of insight into Wayne's fun-loving, laughter-filled ways. Like most of us in the later seasons of life, Wayne had talked of "when I die" many times to family and friends. At some point before he was sick, Wayne had laughingly told Steven, "When I die, if you all plan to file by and look at me in the casket, I'm going to make sure I'm wired to rise up and scare you to death." Little did Wayne know that his fun-loving words would be spoken at his real funeral! Steven, who shares a great sense of humor with his dad, gave a beautiful message and then threw in Wayne's joke. Such a comment was vintage Wayne. For everyone grieving his loss, it was such a sweet reminder of the pastor who loved us and always made us laugh. We all could hear him saying that very thing. How we loved him! He had taught us the grace of Christ, and he had taught us to laugh. How could we not laugh at his Celebration of Life?

During the Civil War that tore this country apart, Abraham Lincoln asked his cabinet, "Gentlemen, why don't you laugh? With the fearful strain that is upon me night and day, if I did not laugh I should die, and you need this medicine as much as I do."[1] Lincoln understood the balance of life. No matter what we are going through, there needs to be a counterbalance of laughter.

Laughter in hard seasons is not something you plan, but it's also not something you avoid. When you see or hear something that strikes you as funny, go ahead and smile, giggle, or laugh out loud. Give yourself the internal permission. It won't change the pain of the season. It won't change the circumstances of the unknown future. But for that moment, the laughter will bring a relief to the stress you're experiencing.

My friend Charlotte was a master of breaking up the hard moments with laughter. She's been gone several years now, but when I think of her, I always laugh. She always brought relief to the moment with one of her quips. Toward the end of her life, when it was clear she wasn't going to recover from her cancer, we continued to chat, as good girlfriends do, about looks and makeup and little repairs we'd like to have done. We both knew she was dying and that it wouldn't be long, but we laughed and talked as if we had years.

One day, she stopped in the middle of our prattle and said very seriously, "See this little bump on my nose?" As I inspected the almost imperceptible flaw, she said, "I'd like to have that taken off." I continued to look, not knowing what to say, when she added, "But you know . . . I probably won't need to have that done." We looked at one another for a split second and then broke out in laughter. She knew exactly what she was doing when she brought up the bump. Being able to laugh together over the absurd made it so much easier to cry together over the real. (This is the same girl who called to tell me there was a documentary on cemeteries on TV, so "be sure and watch!" Really, Charlotte?)

Oh, how I miss her! But even though she's gone, the laughter continues. I'm just sorry she missed her own funeral. She would have loved it. I was honored to speak, and I still remember looking at the faces of her sweet family as they sat in the first two rows at the funeral home. Telling "Charlotte stories" helped bring laughter through the many tears. We all made it through that service, consoled by knowing Charlotte was at Home with the One she had trusted for many years.

The graveside ceremony was almost over when something happened that she would have relished. Everything had been so well done. We had laughed and cried, and now it was time for her body to be laid to rest. It was a beautiful day, and after the last words were spoken, three doves were released and flew away with all the grandeur that such a moment can bring. We all watched them fly into the sun, and I breathed a sigh of relief over the freedom Charlotte now felt. As I took in the moment with such tender feelings, I heard my sweet husband lean over to a friend standing next to him and say quietly, "Too bad it's not hunting season."

What did he just say? I couldn't kick his leg fast enough. I died the death of the mortified as I quietly gasped until I could breathe again. It was then that I had to laugh. Charlotte would have loved it! She would have died laughing. She would have had some smart reply for my husband, and we would have laughed and walked away. It was the thing she did best. She brought humor to the painful, to the sacred, and to the unexpected.

When we laugh in the face of difficult situations, we join a great host of people who have learned that the art of laughter is a gift in any season, especially the painful and unknown. Some of the most awful circumstances that have faced the world were the concentration camps of World War II. Surrounded by death and unthinkable cruelties, some of the camp inmates were able to "rise above," if only for a few minutes, by tapping into their sense of humor. Viktor Frankl was one of those inmates who believed that choosing laughter and a sense of humor, more than anything else, can help us to rise above any situation. And truly, Frankl meant *any* situation. He wrote, "The attempt to develop a sense of humor and to see things in a humorous light is some kind of a trick learned while mastering the art of living. Yet it is possible to practice the art of living even in a concentration camp, although suffering is omnipresent."[2]

Laugh! It's Healthy!
Laughter has an amazing effect on our bodies, especially when we're under stress. It triggers the release of a cascade of chemicals that boost our immune responses, including our antiviral and antitumor defenses. Yes, viruses and tumors are affected by the hormones released when we laugh! NK cells, endorphins, serotonin, growth hormone, interferon gamma (IFN), and a lot of other wonderful stuff pours out if we laugh for an extended period of time. That conglomeration of scientific names may not mean much to you, but any medical professional will tell you that it is a list of "happy juices" that will do you good when they are released in your body. These substances are unlike the not-so-nice cortisol that pours into your body when you are under stress, as we talked about in the last chapter. Laughter is one of our great minimizers of the bad effects of cortisol.

Laughter is like "a little trap door that allows you to escape from toxic stress."[3] It may be a momentary escape, but it is a relief for that moment. When you are in a season that is filled with nothing but stress, having an escape can be a lifesaver.

God gave us this secret about laughter in the book of

Proverbs. Who has not heard Proverbs 17:22: "A merry heart does good, like medicine, but a broken spirit dries the bones" (NKJV)? How glibly we let that one slide off our tongues or glide past our eyes, but the truth this verse contains is incredible. Think about it—why would "medicine" and "bones" be included in a verse about a "merry heart"? Since God wrote the book and created us, He knows what we're made of and what makes us healthy. It's all wrapped up in what we think—believe it or not, what we think affects our bones and so much more. But it starts with bones!

How many of us give much thought to our bones? Do you ever think about what goes on with bones besides weight bearing? Inside those bones is bone marrow, which makes blood cells. We never see it, so we don't think about it, but it's doing its work while we go about our lives reacting, worrying, and ruminating on our circumstances. Sometimes we're merry and sometimes we're gloomy. Sometimes the sun shines and we're happy. Sometimes the clouds roll in and we're depressed. Our thinking goes on while our bone marrow goes about its business making blood cells. We have no idea there's a connection.

Maybe you were sleeping and missed this day in science (like I did), so here's a little catch-up: Blood cells start out as stem cells that make up bone marrow, which is found in our ribs, vertebrae, sternum, and pelvis. These stem cells divide into red blood cells and white blood cells.

Red blood cells carry oxygen and nutrients throughout our bodies, while white blood cells go about fighting infection. But there's more!

Fields of study such as psychoneuroimmunology, or neuroimmunomodulation, are revealing "that stress, depression, sorrow, grief, anger, and negative thoughts have a direct negative effect on white blood cells."[4] Stop and think about that for a minute: Your mind-set has an effect on all those colds and viruses to which you are prone. Now, your mind-set isn't the only contributor, but it has a big impact!

Conversely, your "happy, joyful, restful, positive thoughts have a direct positive effect on white and red blood cell production and activity."[5] And it is even more nuanced than that. The "first line of defense against infectious organisms trying to enter through our respiratory tract is salivary immunoglobulin A," and "confirmed research shows that salivary immunoglobulin A is lower when one is in a negative mood and higher on days when one is in a positive mood."[6] Translation: Your saliva has better protective qualities if you are happy than if you're sad.

So our bones and spit are affected by how we think? Can it be? Well, if God says, "A merry heart does good, like medicine, but a broken spirit dries the bones," then obviously God was telling us something very important in extremely simple terms. While we're reacting and responding to what is going on around us in our emotional lives, our bodies are doing their best to survive. We have the capacity to work with them or against them just by how we think!

A good mood, a cheerful demeanor, a positive thought, a grateful heart, and a smiling face all work toward making a healthier you. Who knew? Negativity can be gratifying; when we go around being cheerless, we tell ourselves that we've let the world know we're not happy about the way things are going. What we seldom factor in is that the world doesn't care! Our families and friends may care, but if we are negative most of the time, they soon chalk that up to "that's just the way she is." It's a no-win situation. Holding on to negative thinking, sour outlooks, self-centeredness, and irritable mind-sets works against us, no matter what season we are going through.

Choosing to have a merry heart is a way to begin helping our bodies. You may say, "I don't feel merry." Maybe there is nothing fun in your life right now. You're in a miserable season.

I understand. I get it. Some would say to "fake it till you make it," but I think your brain, bones, and saliva would know you're faking. They are hard to fool. So choose instead to seek out joy! Seek out laughter!

One place to find joy is in nature. There's always something funny going on with squirrels, kittens, birds, and puppies. Doesn't Jesus say, "When you're worried, consider the birds" (see Luke 12:24)? I think He meant that we should do so because our heavenly Father cares for them—but still, as you consider animals, you can't help but notice their funny little ways.

Trained dogs are allowed to visit nursing homes and be their comforting, funny selves with the patients. Seeing the pups always brings a smile. One of my favorite videos is of a dog nuzzling the hand of a dying woman. Her little hand is gnarled and painfully thin, but her nails are beautifully painted. The dog is on the bed and gently pushes his head up under her hand. She slowly strokes his head with the slightest of movement. It's almost imperceptible, but real nonetheless. As I watched it, I could imagine she must have loved a dog sometime in her life. Maybe having her hand on that dog's head took her back to a sunny day somewhere in her faded memory, and in her heart she smiled. She was close to death, but a faded smile could still bring her a breath of comfort.[7]

Anything that brings a chuckle to your heart will bring health to your bones. Even a small smile in defiance of unpleasant circumstances will start a thought reversal in your head. If you smile once, you can smile again. Keep smiling. Intentionally looking for humor even in unconventional places is a good thing. And if you need to, just laugh out loud. You'll probably find yourself laughing at yourself laughing!

Choosing to smile—to seek laughter when you're going through a hard season—is not easy, but sometimes the road to healing takes many steps. Working on your mind-set is not "woo-woo" medicine. Western medicine has focused so long on chemicals and surgery (and thank goodness it has, as they truly have kept many alive), but sometimes we miss the simple steps that help prevent the disease process in the first place. A merry heart can do wonders!

Join the Parade!
In our ordinary lives lived out in unknown seasons, there are days that seem to be overwhelming. There's too much drama, too many people wanting our attention, or too much bad news in the media. Too much, too much, too much. In many ways, that's life. It's just too much. So at times like this, it's good to remember some advice I saw on a hand-painted sign in a friend's guest room: "If you see a parade, join it!"

Now because of who my friend Betsy is, I knew there had to be a story behind that sign. Betsy laughs easily, loves to roller-skate, and drinks in life with big gulps. On one particular day, she was choking on all of the life she had tried to consume. She had taken on everyone else's burdens as well as her own. She was just plain down. But rather than sit in a dark room and enjoy her misery, she decided to roll her motorcycle out of the garage and go for a ride.

She followed country roads in the east Tennessee hills and came upon a small town that was "fixin' to have a parade." In her downness she had missed the obvious fact it was the Fourth of July. While the parade was gathering, she pulled in behind the last little wagon being pulled by some kids, and when they went forward, she revved her bike up and followed.

Betsy had stuffed her pockets with handfuls of sugar-free hard candy before she left the house. (You never know when you'll need candy!) So she freely threw it to the kids and old folks who waved and yelled as she waved and yelled back. No one in that small town knew who that woman was on the motorcycle! When she reached the end of the parade route, she drove away and headed toward home. Her pockets were empty, but so was the sack of care she had been carrying. She had emptied it as she let herself join in others' joy. She had seen a parade, and she had joined it!

Betsy did exactly what helps when we find ourselves needing healing for our bodies, souls, or spirits. When we are looking for the courage to go through unknown seasons, finding the fun around us matters. Laughter doesn't always come to us. Sometimes we have to go to where it's happening. If you see a sign for a fun event, why not go? You might protest, "Well, I don't know if it will be any good." You'll never know until you go. Sometimes the laughter is in the going! Letting the parades pass by can be to your detriment. So even if you can't join one, be sure to sit on the curb and wave!

CHAPTER FIVE

WHY NOT?

———— ⟨⟨⟨ ————

As long as there's anyone to ask "Why?"
the answer will always be, "Why not?"

VERA NAZARIAN, *The Perpetual Calendar of Inspiration*

"LIFE IS TOO LONG to keep doing things we need to stop, and too short to miss the things we want to begin." Those words came tumbling out of a walk-talk session with my friends Patsy Clairmont and Anita Renfroe as we rambled down the main street of Franklin, Tennessee. The joy the three of us have when we get together needs to be bottled and sold. You probably have friends like that. If not, now is as good a time as any to find some. They don't just happen. You have to be intentional to make and keep good friends!

Due to travel and heavy schedules, the three of us try to make time to meet two or three times a year. Patsy and I are both in our seventies, and Anita is still in her fifties, but we find endless things to discuss and discover. That's what friendship should be as we age. The people we hang out with should be those with whom we can share the journey. That's what Anita, Patsy, and I do for one another—we challenge, affirm, and encourage the hopes and creativity within each of us. That's how new thoughts and greater confidences bubble up. It was these two who said "Go for it!" when I mentioned I wanted to write this book on the unknown seasons.

No matter what unknown season we may find ourselves in, it is imperative to keep a strong sense of adventure alive. Life is to be lived, and the unknown seasons, whether exciting or hard, should never keep us from looking for the life that is around us. There is always something to do or to explore. Too many times, we let the unknown season limit us.

I learned that lesson early on in my adult life. While I now have friends who encourage and inspire me, I once walked through a season when I had no friends around, and I had to look for ways to live on my own. I was twenty-five and was in a new town far from family and friends. My husband had just completed his time in the army as an instructor pilot, and we were transitioning to civilian life in Chattanooga, a place where we knew no one. I was nine months pregnant with our second child (thirty-eight weeks, for those of you who reckon such processes in weeks and not months) when we drove into town with a two-year-old and a hound dog. We quickly moved our few things into the house we had bought, and I went out on the street looking for someone with a baby, hoping he or she could offer the name of an obstetrician. What a season it was! I had no idea how miserable it was until I thought back on it. Glad I was young then. Amazing what we can do when we have to!

After the baby came and we had settled in a little, I became a restless housewife with two little ones under three. I wanted to learn and grow, but I had babies! I found an advertisement for a sewing class at the YWCA downtown. They had a nursery. I thought, *I'm in!*

Three years earlier, for our second Christmas together, my husband had boldly (if not wisely) bought me a sewing machine. Our first baby was born on Saturday, December 23, in an army hospital in a little Texas town. Of course, the stores (such as they were) were closed on Sunday and Christmas Monday, so he was stuck without a Christmas present for me. He quickly went shopping on Tuesday morning before he came to bring us home from the hospital. When it was time to open presents, there it was! He had bought a sewing machine! You can only imagine my thrill: a three-day-old baby, living in a trailer in an army town, not knowing what the unknown season ahead would hold—and he bought a sewing machine. (I can laugh now. I didn't laugh or even have words then, which was probably good!)

So fast-forward three years—we're in Chattanooga, and suddenly I can use my sewing machine! Guess who made herself an Easter dress that year? (Guess who has never sewed another lick on anything?) But for that season, having a sewing machine was so fine. I got out of the house, I attended a class, and I learned something new! I was alive! I had explored a new skill even though it wasn't the best season for it. I was learning. I was reaching out. I was growing. I didn't think to ask "Why not?" back then—I just did it. I think those early adventures into "I'll try this" turned into "I'm going to do this. Why not?"

The thought that our time is too long to keep doing things we need to stop and too short to miss doing things we want to begin has rolled around in my head more than once since Patsy, Anita, and I walked and talked that summer day in Franklin. The stark awareness that time no longer stretches endlessly ahead of me has kept me from taking on projects that could take a lifetime. I could dream up a myriad of things I'd like to still have time to do, like adopting needy kids or buying a horse farm or walking across America, but life is too short for such things, so I confine my desires to lesser projects.

Now it's a new unknown season in my life. Forty-five years have passed since the Christmas of the sewing machine. My boys (we ended up with three) are all grown, and my grandchildren are teenagers. So many seasons have come and gone that it doesn't seem real. Maybe you can relate to how fast it all goes. This past Christmas, I got a dog. (There's something about the Christmas season for me.) It's something I've wanted to do for a long time since our dog Pearl died. She was a passive, quiet soul who basically took up space and ate food, but when she died from cancer after being ours for just five years, I sorely felt her absence. I just like having a dog around. (If you're not a dog lover, don't judge. Just skip over the next few paragraphs, or you'll only roll your eyes.)

As my seventieth birthday (and Christmas) was approaching, I convinced my husband that I really wanted a dog. He wasn't as keen on the idea as I was, but he relented and I began my search. I have inner rules about only adopting dogs that need homes, so I began looking for a rescue. I went to the pet section on Craigslist. After looking and reading and going back over and over again, I saw a picture of a young black-and-white pit bull mix. The caption over his soulful-eyed pose was "The perfect dog for Christmas." He was described as exceptionally smart, playful, and housetrained. The more I looked at his picture, the more I knew he was mine. Again, don't ask me why, because in my head I wanted a female who was older and easygoing—but for this dog I had prayed, and when I saw his picture, well, you know, that was it.

I e-mailed the rescue organization and assumed that one willing inquiry would allow me to pick him up in a day or two. I was so wrong. I found out I had to fill out a twenty-seven-question form and have a home visit in order to be approved as an adoptive dog-mother. I also found out this boy had a checkered past. He was from a town two hundred miles away, had been picked up twice for running the road with an older dog, and had been scheduled to be euthanized. No third chance for him—he was doomed. But wait! A woman from my hometown *happened* to walk into the kill shelter that was holding him and saw my guy playing with a little kitten. Her heart was touched by his gentleness to the point that she called a friend in Chattanooga (where I live) to see if she would help her foster this dog. The friend agreed, and six weeks later, after he had been neutered, immunized, and checked out by the vet, he was on Craigslist. I had no idea about his past or that he had been rescued in the nick of time. All I knew was that for this dog I had prayed. The rest is history.

I've often laughed at myself and this dog. When we first became a team, it reminded me of the character Ouiser and her overgrown dog in the movie *Steel Magnolias*. If you've seen it, that huge dog pulled her all over the little town where the story was staged. My boy, Rocky-Buddy, pulled me everywhere we went for a while. I'd secretly wonder if I had done the right thing and where on earth he was going to pull me next. But then I remembered: *For this dog I had prayed!*

My seventy-first year has been so much fun and so

much more active than it would have been had I not gone ahead and gotten this rambunctious, loving, smart, sweet boy dog. I would not have wanted to miss the joy of having him in my life, although I couldn't have told you what that joy would be. I just knew I wanted a dog, and I didn't want to miss this experience because I didn't think it was the right season.

Every season has its challenges. That's just a fact. As we move from one unknown season to another, we're going to encounter the question "Why not?" And the question that is really being asked is "Why not really live?" There will be different ways of living, depending on your energy, resources, and responsibility. But no matter the season, asking "Why not?" can be a great self-prompter to make the most of whatever comes, even in the unknown season.

What are you not doing because you think it's too late or you don't have enough money or it might be too hard? These can all be blocks to really living. Sometimes you can overcome your self-objections with a little derring-do! Look for short-term adventures if you fear time being too short. Look for free excursions if money is in short supply. Go ahead and meet the challenge, even if it seems really hard.

My friend Ellie Lofaro is a "Why not?" kind of girl. She's always up to an adventure. She recently went on a mission trip to Costa Rica. Afterward I had to smile when she wrote,

The mission trip to Costa Rica was like all mission trips: amazing. As always, we go to give, and we actually get far more than any time, talent, or treasure we think we are bringing to the least of these. It was certainly life changing for me and the others.

And I went on my first zip line! It was over the rain forest. If the cable had broken, they would never have found my body. I thought I would zip along a very long, very high-in-the-sky cable—and I did. What I did not realize was that there would be seventeen more tree platforms and cables to follow. No turning back. No turning back. I felt muscle aches the next day in muscles that have never spoken up nor been seen or heard from before.[1]

But she did it! Why not?

Keep Busy
In the book *70 Things to Do When You Turn 70,* Bob Lowry wrote,

Starting a few years after retirement, things began to change. My routine became too routine. I chafed at what had become a pattern of unfulfilling activities. Too much reading and too many nights spent in front of the television left me feeling empty. For the first time, I began to sense the passage of time.

My days, then weeks, and finally whole months would slip away without my being able to recall accomplishing anything in particular.[2]

No matter our age or season of life, we can fall into the rut of routine. Asking "Why not?" helps us find new life in new seasons. I think of Grandma Moses, the famed folk-art painter who started her huge career in her midseventies. She said, "I have written my life in small sketches, a little today, a little yesterday. . . . I look back on my life as a good day's work, it was done and I feel satisfied with it. I made the best out of what life offered."[3] What life offered was a good husband who was a farm helper, ten children (only five of whom lived past their infancy), time spent being a servant in other people's homes, and debilitating arthritis. It was the arthritis that caused her to give up her beloved embroidery. Then, because she couldn't handle a needle and thread, she began to paint. She loved the colors and hues as she painted the many simple scenes from her life.

At first she sold her pictures for three to five dollars, but then as her fame grew, the prices ranged from five to eight thousand dollars. She became an icon in the art world, but even more, she became known for her resilience. Her attitude was such that had she never picked up a paintbrush, she would have done fine. In fact, she said, "If I didn't start painting, I would have raised chickens."[4] She had advice for everyone on the journey: "Painting's not important. The important thing is keepin' busy."[5] She "kept busy" until she died at 101.

My friend Patsy has decided "keepin' busy" would work for her, too. She has been a speaker with Women of Faith ever since it began in 1996. She has mastered the art of communication and mesmerized audiences with her stories, her humor, and her poignant applications. Everyone knew she was a great speaker, but no one knew what else was in her. When she began to explore art in the last couple of years, all manner of creative delights came tumbling out. She went to a class with a teacher who encouraged her creativity, and now she is a prolific painter.[6]

All of this happened at the end of her sixties and the beginning of her seventies. She never would have known what was in her if she hadn't picked up that paintbrush and dared to put paint on a canvas. Since watching Patsy begin to paint, Anita and I have started painting as well. Now we're not only Shopping Sisters but Palette Pals, too! We paint our pictures and text photos of them back and forth for critiquing. You have to be close to do that. We believe friends are there to cheer each other on to do what they love doing!

All it takes is making the first step. If you want to paint, paint! If you want to write, start writing! Don't be afraid of the judges who always have opinions, and don't bother looking around hoping others will "get it." You are not doing it for others. You are stepping out into a new and unexplored world for yourself! So go ahead!

My friends Chance and Jennifer decided to buy a big used recreational vehicle, bringing their work along with them while they took their girls on adventure trips. It was a creative escapade with all kinds of challenges and joys. In order to do it, they had to ask themselves "Why not?"

My friend Pat, a single mother and grandmother, was living in Texas while her kids were living in California. They wanted her to live close to them. After thinking things through, she decided to sell her house and move. Was it a big undertaking? Absolutely. Were there challenges? You bet. But she wanted to live close to her kids, and in order to do that, she had to move. It's a new, unknown season, but she had to ask herself "Why not?"

What do you want to do that you've been holding back on? What have you always wanted to try that you just haven't gotten around to, and now you're too busy or it may seem too late? Well, it's not! It's time to pick up a brush or pen or call a travel agent or take a course in gourmet cooking or maybe even sewing (did I say that?) and do what you've always wanted to do. There will come an unknown season when you can't pursue the things you would like because of physical limitations, but as long as you can, ask yourself "Why not?"

Don't Count Yourself Out

You may be reading this chapter thinking, *That's fine for others, but I'm not very creative or adventuresome.* My friend, you won't have a clue about what's in you until you actually do something you want to do! If something fascinates you or you've always thought you'd like to try it, then why not? What are you waiting for?

Have you ever thought of using your skills of observation to paint a picture only you can imagine or to put together a story only you can see? Have you shared it with another person and loved the fact that you were the only ones who knew what was going on?

I had such an experience last year at a time I needed to find encouragement wherever I could. I was without my voice for several months due to a surgical procedure that left me with a paralyzed vocal cord. Talk about an unknown season! Not knowing what would happen and not being able to do a lot of communicating with my voice, I quietly went about the things I needed to do.

I wasn't looking for a story, but then I saw the tree. It was just outside the door to the grocery store where I shop. It was skinny, bent over, and broken. It appeared a car had hit it hard. Somehow, though, it had managed to live, and its leaves were luscious and colorful. I observed this with a certain wonder and appreciation for this tree's tenacity. I, too, was having to reach down deep inside myself for tenacity as I coped. I silently cheered that tree on, and I felt there was a message for me in its struggle. Its very existence spoke of living life, no matter how broken and bent by circumstances you might be.

At the same time, I met a young man who worked in the grocery store and was an English major in college. We chatted and I found out he wanted to be a writer, so I told him about the tree and encouraged him to watch it because there was a story there.

I returned to the store several times without seeing him, and then one day, when I was not feeling particularly well, I went through his checkout line. I didn't have much to say but the usual raspy, "Hi, how are you doing? How's school?" As I gathered my groceries and began to leave the line, the gentle college kid said, "The tree still lives." His words were like warm honey pouring over my soul. He had taken note, and now there were two of us watching this broken little tree struggle to survive.

We made it through the winter, and then came early spring. New leaves appeared, even in the broken places, and the next time I saw my college guy, we both smiled and said to one another, "The tree still lives." It just made me happy. I grew to love that tree for its capacity to survive.

Several weeks later, an older guy was taking my groceries to the car, and I asked him if he had noticed my tree. He said no, so since I was parked not too far from where it was, I suggested that we walk over and see it. I thought he'd be encouraged by observing it too. I had just finished telling him the story of the tree "that still lives!" when I looked and was shocked to see that the tree had been cut down. There was nothing there. All that remained was a pile of dirt.

I couldn't believe it. I told the man, "This really makes me mad, and it makes me sad." I'm sure he wondered how soon he could get my groceries into my trunk and send me on my way. Of course, he didn't know all my musings on the resilience and stamina of that dear tree, but he was appropriately moved by my shock as he quickly loaded my groceries into the trunk. I asked him to tell my young friend in the store, "The tree is dead." I said, "He'll understand what you mean." I drove home sickened that someone thought the tree needed to go.

I continued to look at the mound of dirt every time I went by on my way into the store. Finally I told myself, *This is enough grieving over the tree. It's gone. Let it go.* So I just quit looking.

Then summer came. One day I glanced at the patch of ground that had been the black grave of the little tree I had loved, and I couldn't believe my eyes. A shoot about a foot high with green leaves had come up and was alive where the sad, broken tree had been. *The tree still lives!* I said to myself. I couldn't believe it. I snapped a picture as I had done at every stage of the tree's life. It had a story. I knew it, and I wanted a record of how that tree had overcome.

I couldn't wait to dash into the store to find my young writer friend. As I went in the front door, there he was. I grinned broadly as I said, "You're not going to believe this. Have you looked lately? The tree still lives." He laughed with me, and we shared a moment of pure joy. We had observed. We had entered into the story. We had become friends around a broken tree we thought had been axed. And with the appearance of the shoot with new foliage, the sad story became a tale for us both to enjoy! Don't count out a survivor. The tree still lives!

That bent and broken little tree lived to produce leaves in another season. I observed something that I'm fairly certain no one else was watching, but in that tree there was a story for me of overcoming tough circumstances. I invited another person to share, and we did.

People, like trees, can be inspirational and give us creative ideas about what we can explore when the odds don't seem to be in our favor. I always laugh when I think of my friend Suzanne, who began pursuing her PhD at the age of sixty-seven. Knowing it was a three-year pursuit, many of her friends asked her if she knew how old she would be when she got her degree. Suzanne always blew off their questions with her characteristic chuckle, quipping, "The same age I'll be if I don't get it!" It was an unlikely quest that she pursued with joy. She has her doctorate now, is working at several jobs she enjoys, and is loving every minute of her new, challenging, unknown season.

I remember her mantra often as I start on some unlikely adventures in my seventies, including researching and writing this book! Age is really not an issue. I'll be as old as I am whenever I do anything. So it really doesn't matter. The main thing is to ask yourself "Why not?" and just do it!

My parents were never afraid of "just doing it" and, if it didn't work, "just undoing it." When they retired from government work and teaching, they decided to buy a house on a lake in Alabama, about four hours from where my family was settled. It was a great little house, and the waterfront seemed perfect. The boat they parked in the slip attached to the dock was always inviting. My boys were young, and they loved going to Nana and Papa's at the lake. The problem was that Nana and Papa weren't ready to stop working and hang around the lake. They had never been water people, and the allure of living the life of retirees on the lake soon lost its glitter.

A US senator had an office in the nearby town of Tuscumbia. He was coming up for reelection, so my parents decided to volunteer for his campaign. He was a wonderful, well-respected former judge, and my parents felt that their time could be better spent helping him get reelected than sitting around the lake.

It wasn't long before they were in their second careers— in their seventies! My dad's accounting skills and my mother's people skills soon found both of them full-time employment in Senator Howell Heflin's office. They thrived on the work and the mental stimulation. I think it mattered to them that they still mattered. They soon sold the lake house, moved into town, and happily went to work every day for several more years. My dad had to stop first as his health failed, but my mother kept working until it was clear she needed to come home and deal with the aging process in my dad and ultimately in herself.

I've always loved having their example of not being afraid to "just undo it." They thought their unknown season was going to be life on the lake as retirees, but it didn't work for them—so they put up the for-sale sign and moved to town to go in another direction. That was definitely an unknown season, but it worked for them. Some people probably thought they were crazy, but I can see those two looking at one another, shrugging, and saying "Why not?"

Because we don't know the future, we have to do things based on the knowledge we have at the time. So we can never make a perfect decision. But if there's not a check in your spirit and it's not clearly a foolish or illegal move, then why not go for something you've always wanted to do and would seemingly energize you?

Be Curious and Intentional
Maybe you're not sure what you would like to do or even what you could do. This is when I encourage people to stir up their curiosity. Begin to ask questions and look for answers. Curiosity will lead you to explore some things you've never thought about before. With information so readily available on the Internet, there's no excuse for not asking questions! That's the path to keeping your mind young and staying in touch with a world that is changing

faster than we can imagine. If you can google any question you might ever have and find an answer, then your learning potential is limited only by what you can imagine asking.

In this day and time, there's no reason to be uneducated about all the ins and outs of the unknown seasons of life. Whatever lies ahead, you can explore! With access to computers, we can know anything we want to know and be the best-educated generation of people to come along. If you want to know it, look it up and get the details! No need to sit and wonder what to do about almost anything.

I love asking questions about household chores that have stymied me. Just last night I googled how to make a granite counter really shiny. Between the time I shut down my computer and the time I went to bed, I applied what I had learned, and my countertops came out sparkling. It doesn't take much to entertain me, but I freely admit I love learning anything new—and Google is my go-to answer man!

Curiosity can take you way beyond Google when you begin to think of the things you'd really like to do before you breathe your last. Even if your money is limited, there is so much you can pursue if you just allow your creative juices to flow and follow the paths where your curiosity takes you.

I recently read about an interesting woman who followed her curious bent. Phoebe was an avid birder who was diagnosed with terminal cancer right before her fiftieth birthday. She had been watching birds for years with great joy. Not to be daunted by her diagnosis, she decided to expand her "life list," a term birders use for the ongoing pursuit of differing species of exotic birds. She traveled with abandon to more and more distant and exotic places to see *rarae aves* (rare birds). Her cancer went into remission, and she kept going. By the time she died at age sixty-eight, she had seen a record 8,400 species, thought to be 85 percent of the world's known birds. Although Phoebe and other birders call their pursuit of seeing birds their "life list," they really mean things they want to experience while they still have time[7]—something we all need to think about!

The idea of the "life list" was translated to the more familiar "bucket list," made famous by the movie of the same name. Morgan Freeman and Jack Nicholson starred as two older men who found out they were terminally ill and set out to do what they had dreamed of doing before they "kicked the bucket." Over the past years, I've heard more and more people, old or not, say that going there or doing that is "on my bucket list." I think it's a good idea to have such a list, because if we're not intentional about doing the things we've always wanted to do, when will we get them done?

What's on your bucket list? What do you want to do, see, or be before it's your time to die? It may be as simple as cake decorating or gourmet cooking. You may want to take a class in how to master your Mac. Maybe you've always wanted to take a cruise or travel by RV across America. It could be you want to do some genealogical work to find out where you've come from, or you may want to visit the old country where the graves of your ancestors are located. Of course, there's always a visit to the Holy Land, where your spiritual roots go deep.

Writing a journal can be fun too. Journals are wonderful to revisit as the years pass by. I've seen some of my own journaling from middle school and have been amazed that the dreams I dreamed are pretty close to the way life turned out. My daughter-in-law has prolifically journaled the life and times of her children. She has very thick books packed with memories of their lives. I'm sure they've never looked at them, but someday, they will love all that their mother has done to record their life history.

My mother was a journaler of sorts. She didn't write prolifically, but she kept a calendar where she recorded events, thoughts, birthdays, doctor's visits, and hospitalizations. While my dad was sick with dementia, Mother kept succinct records of his decline. After she died, it was interesting and poignant to look back through her handwritten notes that chronicled that time in my parents' lives.

The main thing we have to choose in life is intentionality. Haphazard living and just waiting for life to happen will leave us in a very compromised place.

Even when you're older, not letting age stop you from the things you want is critical to living intentionally. A doctor friend told me about preparing to go on a mission trip with a wonderful gentleman who had some heart problems. The doctor asked him if he was sure he should go, considering his condition. The hearty traveler said, "I have to die somewhere!"

The doctor asked him what he wanted him to do if his heart gave out on the trip. "Just bury me in the land and tell my sweet wife where you put me," the man said. That took care of that! The next question could only be "Why not?" They took the trip and ministered to the people he was sent to love. That was several years ago, and he's still going.

Dr. Louis and Anne Carter are in their midseventies. For many years, several times a year, they have traveled to Africa to perform surgery on people with diseased, injured, and malformed limbs and faces. These people would go untreated were it not for the Carters' work. Although Louis and Anne have been on and off the mission field for more than forty years, the thought of retirement just doesn't occur to them. They're always planning the next trip—even if it is in between their own surgeries and rehabs. "Why not?" seems to be their theme. Why stop now?

When you look back on your life, you're going to want to say, "I took advantage of every opportunity that was put in front of me. I didn't make excuses." Excuses are usually our way of escape. If you don't want to do something, be honest about it and say, "Thanks, but I really don't want to do that." That seems to be a hard thing for some of us to say, but it's okay not to want to do something. If your motives are purely based on your desires and not your fears or prejudices, it's really okay. If, however, you would like to do something but you are adept at talking yourself out of it, then that's another story. Making excuses takes the verve out of your spirit. If you let yourself off the hook too easily, you will probably live to regret it. In your young seasons, you'll encounter many unknowns, but stay true to the creative adventurer in you and don't let the circumstances dull your joy for the journey. Even if it is a small adventure, go for it.

When Charlie and I were newlyweds, we lived in an old house that had been divided into apartments. We were twenty-two and twenty-three years old, and the other tenants were in their eighties. Miss Mae Mink lived downstairs and loved to keep our puppy for us. She loved dogs, and our little dog, Andy, had a place with her anytime we wanted to share him. In fact, we really weren't supposed to have a dog, but Miss Mae did her best to help us keep him under wraps. (No judgment, please!) We got him just three weeks before we were moving, so she stepped into the adventure and loved it!

Across the hall from us was Mr. Vincent Brigalli, a retired violinist. Some nights, he would come in to visit and play his violin. He was a lonely man who found an audience in the young newlyweds across the hall. Talking with him wasn't that easy, but when he would lift his violin to play, he communicated in ways that were unmistakable. He played beautifully, and we enjoyed his visits.

We all were in such different times of life and were headed into unknown seasons. Miss Mae and Mr. Vincent had lived their lives, and we were just beginning to live ours. When we moved we never saw them again, but we remember them for their sparkle and their love of life. Miss Mae loved dogs. Mr. Vincent loved his music. They both taught us much about living in a season we knew nothing about. We were young and clueless, engulfed in the fog of our newlywed spring. We had no idea about a winter season, although now we do! We've figured out a few things, one of which is that these are the years to do what you want to do. There's no more time for excuses and hesitations.

It really doesn't matter what you set out to do, but it matters *that* you decide to do! Wishing, thinking, and pondering hold no satisfaction. If you want to do something, ask yourself the question "Why not?" If you can really come up with a reason why you shouldn't, then set it aside for a while and revisit it. Sometimes things look better after you've had time to sleep on them. Don't automatically throw ideas away; just give yourself time to let the dust settle, and maybe then you will see more clearly. It may be a matter of time, or it may be a bad idea. You'll never know until you ask yourself that all-important question: "Why not?"

CHAPTER SIX

LETTING GO

———⟨∞⟩———

Some of us think holding on makes us strong;
but sometimes it is letting go.

HERMANN HESSE

WHEN UNEXPECTED and unwanted changes come into your world, it usually means you will be required to let go, to release your grip, to accept what has happened. Yet in your heart, you may have a need to hold tight, to hang on. Your greatest longing is probably for the unwanted change not to be permanent. You may have a wistful hope of returning to the way things were, and that hope may linger even after irreversible change has occurred.

And yet those changes still do come in the most painful and profound ways.

Your spouse becomes terminally ill in body or in mind. The eyes that once lit up when you came in the room are lifeless as they watch you come near his bed. Life as you once knew it is over.

Your child who couldn't hug and kiss you enough when she was a little girl is now estranged as a young woman. The coldness in her eyes says, "Don't come near me." Your heart shrinks back. Where did she go?

You've been diagnosed with cancer and are facing chemotherapy and radiation treatments. You long to return to yesterday, to before you heard the diagnosis, but you can't. You have to move forward to fight a fight you never asked for.

Your best friend moves away. She's not moving back. You can't hang on to the comfort of her being next door anymore. A stranger will live there now.

Your church is no longer a hymn-singing, dress-up-for-Sunday kind of sanctuary that you loved. It's now a worship-song-singing, candles-and-sandals meeting place that doesn't feel like home anymore. The hymnbooks are in the maintenance closet and the music is on the wall, and there's no going back.

When change comes to the people and places you thought would never change, it's normal to want to hang on. You're not sure what you're hanging on to, but the familiar gives you a sense of security. Somehow it feels as if you won't have to let go if you try to keep hanging on. But usually when we have to let go, it's because what we loved and found familiar just doesn't exist anymore.

When the hard changes come, how can you affirm to yourself that you really did have another life? How can you believe that it was good and productive while also believing that the very different life you're living today is just as good?

My friends Steve and Pam were a picture of letting go while hanging on. Pam had a lung disease that took her to the edge of death before she received a transplant. In an emergency flight to Cleveland Clinic, it was evident Pam probably would not make it. In fact, before Pam boarded the flight, the doctor told this long-married couple that they might want to say their good-byes in case she didn't survive the flight. Amazingly, Pam made it to Cleveland, where she had the surgery. After many months of struggle, she and Steve returned to their home in Tennessee, and Steve, who had been with her every day of her hospitalization, took on the role of her caretaker. For three years, he cheered her on and did everything possible to enable her to hang on to life. He knew she was slipping away, but he wasn't going to count her out until she was gone. Her situation grew worse, and another emergency flight took her back to Cleveland Clinic. For three agonizing weeks, Steve prayed and hoped and urged Pam to keep trying to live—to please, please hang on—but she just couldn't. She wanted desperately to let go.

I saw them for a brief visit during that time in the ICU. As I walked into the tiny cubicle full of life support

equipment, I saw a husband in tears and a wife struggling to breathe. Her face was covered with a full oxygen mask from her forehead to her chin. The medical
people had told them that she was going to be intubated
shortly, which meant she wouldn't be able to talk, so they
were saying their last words before things changed again.
They didn't know how long they had. They didn't know
what other decisions they would have to make. They just
didn't know anything for sure, but they did know this
season was bringing them closer and closer to letting
go—forever.

Pam was eager to leave. Her fight to breathe had become
too much, and while Steve couldn't stand to watch her suffer, he still wanted her to stay. He was letting go with his
head, but his heart cried out for Pam to "keep trying, keep
going!" He wanted to hang on.

A few days later, Steve called me and said, "Well, I
think the time has come." All efforts had failed. So with
their two children holding Pam's hands, Steve prayed and
quietly read from the Scriptures:

Who shall separate us from the love of Christ?
Shall tribulation, or distress, or persecution, or
famine, or nakedness, or peril, or sword? . . . For
I am persuaded that neither death nor life, nor
angels nor principalities nor powers, nor things
present nor things to come, nor height nor depth,

nor any other created thing, shall be able to
separate us from the love of God which is in Christ
Jesus our Lord.

ROMANS 8:35, 38-39, NKJV

Their final day together had come. Pam breathed her
last labored breath and was gone. Steve had to loosen his
emotional grip as the finality of her loss became a reality.
There was no longer any way to hang on. She was gone,
and there was no returning.

Life teaches that there are many nuances to letting go.
Seasons roll by day by day, and as we mature, we learn that
life really is one big exercise in letting go. Even if we're in
a time when we believe we can't bear to let go, inside we
know that every season only lasts for a while. Soon another
change and another season will come.

If you and I are honest, in our hearts we usually equate
the idea of "letting go" with sadness and pain. But it
doesn't always have to be that way. Emotional struggle is
just that—a struggle, not a finality. It is in refusing to
loosen our grip that the greatest struggles come. Once we
let go, or the objects of our affections have moved away or
faded from our immediate attention, the skies clear and
new possibilities come into view—if we let them. It is the
process of passing time that opens the door for this to
happen.

But, you may ask, what about Pam and Steve? How

can anything new come out of such a sad experience that ended in separation and death? Well, God has His ways, if we are open to them. As Pam breathed her last on this earth, she opened her eyes in a realm of experience none of us can begin to know or describe. I love these words that come back to me every time I hear of the passing of someone who lived by faith:

Just think of stepping on shore
And finding it heaven,
Of touching a hand and finding it God's
Of breathing new air and finding it celestial
Of waking up in glory and finding it home.[1]

Pam left behind a lot of earthly suffering that had made her life more and more unsustainable. She finally let go of earth's air and woke up in a new atmosphere of easy breathing. She arrived at home. We won't know what that looks, feels, and smells like until we're there, but this much I know: Pam could not be more Pam, more alive, more free, and more delighted than she is at this moment.

Steve went through a year of putting his life in order after years of total attention to the needs of a dying wife. He built a man cave in his home. Because his relationship with Pam civilized him to the ways of making a house beautiful, his idea of a man cave was very woman friendly. It's a good thing—because Steve has now remarried. Pam always will be remembered, respected, and dearly loved, but when she left her earthly body, Steve let go of her. And in due time, through tears of grief, he let go of being her husband. He took on a new role and emerged into a spacious new area where new experiences and new people could exist in his life. Gwen Tatum McCary is now his wife.[2] As Bryant H. McGill once said, "Abundance is a process of letting go; that which is empty can receive."

As we talked about in the beginning of this chapter, not all our letting gos involve death of the earthly body. Sometimes it's the good-byes that come with children growing up and leaving home, or parents aging, or friends moving, or relationships losing steam, or expectations going unfulfilled, or our own bodies becoming less energetic.

There are so many times in life when it would seem so much better to hang on to what was than to let go and find out what might be. Often what's waiting is such a mystery that we can't believe there is anything on the other side of what has changed. Yet we cannot hang on to what no longer exists and still expect to live life as God designed. It's critical to get hold of the fact that God dwells only in what is real, not in what we wish could be. Understanding this helps us face the truth of how we handle the unknown seasons of life.

How about you? Are you living in a world of "what used to be"? Or is it a world of "I wish things were different"? Do you look back and do more reminiscing than looking to what is happening today? Do you look forward, yearning for what you might be in the future? The reality is that "the good old days" and "what might be" don't exist. Today is it! Today is the space you inhabit with God. He is the I AM of your today. He lived in the past, He lives today, and He does inhabit your future—but *you* live today! The past is gone and you haven't lived tomorrow yet, so your time is pretty closely defined by *right now*. To squander what's in your hand will only bring a loss to you and those around you at the end of the day. So what are you doing with "now"? Are you fully absorbing the "today" that is? Asking yourself these questions every day will keep you centered.

If you let your mind wander to what's going to happen, you're confronted with two paths: You either will find the path of dread that leads to worry or the path of anticipation that often leads to disappointment. Neither path is reality. We worry about things that are not as bad as we imagine, and we anticipate future experiences that often leave us empty. Absorbing ourselves in the joys of the present day is really the only authentic place to settle.

Life lived *in* the moment requires intentional focus *on* the moment. It is so easy for our minds to wander. You know how it feels—you want to be in the moment with your kids or a friend or with the Lord, but you find your mind wandering. *What did she mean by what she said? What's going to happen next week? I wish I'd said something different when he brought up the money.* The list is unending. Any shiny thought can capture our attention, and when it does, we are pulled away from the moment.

Jesus had to keep His disciples focused on the moment as well.

> Don't be concerned about what to eat and what
> to drink. Don't worry about such things. These
> things dominate the thoughts of unbelievers all
> over the world, but your Father already knows
> your needs. Seek the Kingdom of God above all
> else, and he will give you everything you need.
>
> So don't be afraid, little flock. For it gives your
> Father great happiness to give you the Kingdom.
>
> LUKE 12:29-32, NLT

I think Jesus hit the nail on the head (of course He would) in helping us think about living today: Don't be afraid! Your Father delights in giving you all you need, when you need it, so pay attention to what you're about today. That is where your Father is working.

I have a friend who is the sole caretaker for her mother, who has advanced Alzheimer's disease. My friend has been a successful career woman. Today, she cares for a woman who doesn't know who she is. She spends her days making sure her mother is clean, safe, and fed. Either that is all one big mistake and the fulfillment of my friend's worst fear, or it is the place where God dwells in her life—today. She can look back and pine for the days when her mother could care for herself, or she can look forward to the days when her mother is no longer on this earth to be cared for—or she can say to herself, "This is where God has me, and He is in this day. He was with me yesterday. I'm grateful. He'll be with me tomorrow, and I thank Him, but my reality—and His reality in my life—is today! Where can I see Him? What purpose might He have? Can I trust Him that this season is not forever? Can I know that He is at work in all of this?" This is when the definition of faith from Hebrews 11:1 is either true or it's not: "Faith is confidence in what we hope for and assurance about what we do not see" (Hebrews 11:1, NIV).

The reality of life happens in the moment, and the moment you are alive is now. Gloria Gaither, poet and songwriter, has said it so well: "Everything is a part of what God's up to in your life so I think our job is to embrace it. Everything. Embrace it all and consider it God's will for this moment."[3]

Now, "embracing" the good, bad, and ugly in your life doesn't mean that you passively experience life as a victim of some imperial God who plays you like a puppet. It does mean that you look beyond the event to the good hand of the God who loves you, and you seek with wonder His holy presence and plan in all that is occurring. He doesn't always say yes to our heartfelt prayers for healing or redemption or even for rain in a time of drought, but somehow, someway, when the circumstances seem to be too big for us to conquer, He gives us Himself in another way.

Because we see with earthly eyes, we expect God to work in earthly ways—and yet to know Him is to truly believe that His ways are not our ways. To trust Him is to believe with all our hearts that He is good, His ways for us are for our good, and His plans are far beyond what we can conceive. Often, it is His presence that brings wonder to our day. Even when circumstances have brought changes we find hard to embrace, the presence of the Holy One allows us to loosen our grip on our earthly beloved and with trembling hearts embrace the "what is" of the moment.

Brother Lawrence was a man who learned the secret of living in the presence of God on a moment-by-moment basis, no matter the circumstances. He lived in the 1600s, and after a career as a soldier and a brief stint as a government worker, he found himself at midlife working as a cook in a monastic community. It was there he learned to wash dishes (although he hated it) "as unto the Lord." An admirer of his wrote in typical sixteenth-century verbiage, "When an occasion of practising some virtue offered, he addressed himself to GOD, saying, LORD, I cannot do this unless Thou enablest me; and . . . then he received strength more than sufficient. . . . We ought to act with GOD in the greatest simplicity, speaking to Him frankly and plainly, and imploring His assistance in our affairs, just as they happen. . . . GOD never failed to grant it."[4]

Grant what? His presence in whatever was going on, just as it happened! The moment-by-moment presence of God makes today significant. And God is working in the moment by moment of your day.

What does that have to do with letting go while wanting to hang on? Everything. This is not a journey we make alone. We have been promised the gift and presence of the Holy Spirit in our lives. He is our guide, our teacher, and our comforter through whatever we must walk on this earth. Whether we are experiencing the most difficult days we have known to date or we are "washing dishes" in a mundane situation that seems endless, God the Holy Spirit is with us in every moment. He is a breath away, whether we call to Him with a little whimpering prayer or with a deep, guttural sob. He occupies the moment in which we are living, and He has no intention of leaving us alone. That is what makes it possible to let go even when our hearts cry out to hold on.

The beautiful transaction that takes place in this moment is the holy recognition that God knows your name, He knows where you are, and He knows that you want to hang on to what gave you comfort, to where you felt important, to what you loved. Seeking security in the way things were is our human way of grasping for comfort. Letting go of comfort and embracing the awkward newness of things as they are is an act of faith. It is living in the moment, trusting the God who occupies the moment.

As you work through "letting go" while longing to hang on in your own life, make a note of where you have seen and felt the presence of God. Have your needs been met? Has He come alongside and blessed you in ways you didn't expect? Have you sensed that when you let go, something else will be put in your hand? Could it be that as you release your grip on the familiar, you are going to experience the very presence of God?

CHAPTER SEVEN

HEAD TOWARD NINETY

⁓⏦⁓

Stay calm and keep aging!
ANONYMOUS

"**IT FEELS AS IF THE GHOST** of fear is sneaking around outside the door, looking for a chance to come in and get a grip." A friend of mine wrote these words about the approach of a new season in her life. At the age of seventy-one, she has gone through her share of annoying physical inconveniences. I can tell they have chipped away at some of her self-confidence, but I know her—she's not the type to stay in a state of uncertainty. She is pursuing every avenue of strengthening and age delay she can find, even though she's fully aware that the winter season is approaching with some chilly winds.

Living well in the winter season takes time, effort, and

sometimes a change in some old habits, but the alternative is to sit down and wait for the ravages of winter and the ghost of fear to form an alliance to take over your life. That is a terrifying prospect for most of us, and yet it's a given if we don't approach the chill of growing older with an eye toward doing what we can for ourselves. This is true whether you are forty, fifty, sixty, or seventy. If you are feeling physically challenged with some of the things you are seeing in your own life, now is a good time to wake up and take charge of the process. You can't stop aging, but you can delay the process with some simple steps.

The recognition that we're not as young as we used to be is so cliché, but it's true. No one is as young as he or she was a minute ago. No one stands still in a favorite spot on the calendar forever. Inevitably, time moves on whether we want to move with it or not. The aging process is relentless, but if we meet it with some common sense and sharp medical interventions on the simplest level, it can be smoother.

We who are at the vanguard of the boomer generation are best served if we learn as much as we can about the things we can do to ward off the ills and inconveniences of the years. You who are gen Xers are not that far behind, so it's a good thing to pay attention.

Prepare to Be Healthy

I've always loved medical information. As a ten-year-old child, I often visited the National Museum of Health and

Medicine in Washington, DC, where I lived. I can remember standing and looking with wonder in the display cases as I saw fascinating specimens preserved for scientific study. I saw engorged legs that had been removed due to elephantiasis, along with diseased lungs, deformed hands, and malformed hearts all preserved in jars of formaldehyde for study. I loved trying to figure out what had gone wrong. I know, I know. I was probably an odd child by most standards since I loved visiting the medical museum more than watching cartoons. Not much has changed. I still like to observe and learn all I can.

Fortunately, my work office is located in a wonderful place that allows me the privilege of observing, listening, and learning from an internist of uncommon knowledge and skill. His name is Dr. Kerry Friesen. He has been in practice for more than twenty-five years and is a born teacher. Just being around him is a valuable classroom experience. He loves to explain the why behind what is going on in our bodies, and he stays up on all the latest information. He's not bound to a prescription pad and a pen. He does prescribe pharmaceuticals when warranted, but he is equally invested in prescribing natural supplements that can strengthen and sustain our brains and bodies.

Prevention is a major theme with Dr. Friesen. He is on the cutting edge of telling us how to ward off or lessen the impact of certain maladies. He never prescribes a ridiculous

Spartan diet or hard-core exercise, thank goodness. Instead, he gives common sense and often little-known remedies that can make all the difference in a lifestyle.

Just the other day he told me, "All thirty-seven trillion cells that make up our exquisitely designed bodies are renewed every seven years. So a baby is born with one set of cells, and by the time he reaches age seven, he has a completely new set of cells. The same is true at fourteen, twenty-one, twenty-eight, thirty-five, forty-two, and on and on." So, boomers who are turning seventy are a whole new set of cells getting ready to start a new part of the journey. And for gen Xers who are in their forties, the newest cellular changes have brought on some twists in the journey. Your eyes have begun to change, and the reading glasses come out. You may begin to notice other changes that weren't there just a few years ago.

You may feel a little slower, a little less energetic, or not quite as flexible as you have been. All that renewing that is going on is slowing down, too, because each individual cell is going about its business in a slower, more age-appropriate pace! So as we turn forty-nine, fifty-six, sixty-three, seventy, and seventy-seven, the cells are being renewed, but they aren't the cells of our youth. They are the cells that make a forty-nine-year-old instead of a forty-two-year-old, or of a thirty-five-year-old and not a twenty-eight-year-old. The changes have been happening all along, but some dates make you particularly aware. Seventy, if you are there, is one of those dates. And if you're not there, then hang on, sweetheart, you will be!

I heard where one seventy-year-old woman was talking with her doctor after surviving the ravages of cancer and chemotherapy. Looking for advice from him about how to conduct the rest of her life, she was surprised when he said, "Head toward ninety!" I think that's a great motto for all of us: Let's just head toward ninety! If we don't make it, we don't, but if we do, then good for us! I have a ninety-year-old aunt who is quite pleased that she can still drive and "get in and out of the bathtub with no trouble!" I say hurrah for you, Aunt Jane! Why not? If you can, you should!

In order to head toward ninety, there are some simple but significant things we can do or undo in our lives to delay aging. Life-changing health habits are teeming (but hidden) within the pages of thousands of medical journals, and Dr. Friesen has spent a lifetime gathering this information so you don't have to. He has shared these ideas with me along the way, and I've always been gratefully amazed at how simple some of these steps can be. If you are bored with the "exercise and watch your diet" advice that seems to be as deep as some providers can go, then you'll appreciate the simplicity and kindness that comes with the following insights. (That's one of the joys that comes with age: We can push back and say to our younger, haven't-been-there-yet medical professionals, "Don't you have something more creative than that to offer?")

Exercise

Dr. Friesen has never been one to fuss about weight, and yet by following some of his simple suggestions, I lost twenty pounds without trying. His exercise recommendations for boomers entering the winter season is to major on stretching and weight bearing.

"Don't go knock yourself out on treadmills or in hardcore cardio exercise," he told me. "You beat yourself up and get joint strains that only will cause you pain. Stretch, stretch, stretch. Pick up heavy things. Keep the strength in your upper legs and arms. That will do more to help you age with strength than any other exercises you can do."

I well remember ten years ago when he said, "If you want to stay out of a nursing home, keep your upper legs strong." Then he demonstrated by standing from a sitting position without using his hands. That one simple exercise can keep you mobile. If you can't get up from a seated position, you will be limited. Try it. You'll see it's not easy, but it is doable. If you're not there yet, you can get there with some practice.

Another thing we need to pay attention to in the exercise department is how much we're sitting. Lengthy sitting is the new smoking. Our bodies were not meant to sit, sit, sit. Eventually, we'll pay the price for our long-term "sit-ins." My good doctor, who has taught me so much over the years, says, "Ten minutes, anytime, anywhere." That means to make it a point to move for ten minutes as often as you can. If you are on a plane for several hours or riding in your car or at a desk or enjoying your favorite lounge chair, make it a point to get up and move! If you're like me, you assume you have to go for a long walk or go to the gym or do something that's going to take a lot of time to get in the movement you need. But the good news is "Ten minutes anytime, anywhere" is enough. We can do this! In fact, I think it's time for me to get up. I've been sitting here writing way too long. Let's both get up and stretch. Now's the time, and wherever you are is the place!

Falls

Falls are such a hazard in the aging process. Despite our lithe and facile ways during our youth, those cellular changes every seven years can make a real difference in balance once we reach our sixties, seventies, and eighties. Medications, blood pressure issues, neurological changes, inner ear problems, and impaired eyesight can work against us staying upright. Not to mention rugs, cats, dogs, and other household hazards! Knowing all of this, we need to make sure we hang on to railings and wear sensible shoes. I know it sounds old fashioned and simple, but awareness is one of the best fall preventatives there is.

I love my friend Luci Swindoll. She is eighty-four now, but when she was eighty she told me with a smile, "I don't move fast. My friends don't like the speed I go, but I haven't fallen yet." Luci has faced her years with grace and has made compensation for the toll they've taken. There's nothing demeaning about facing where we are and bowing to the need to move a little differently. Awareness is the key to moving safely, which is why Luci has modified her life to move slowly and more deliberately. When you stand up to start walking, being deliberate is important. Stand for a few seconds, make sure you're balanced, and then walk. "Bowing to age" sometimes means not falling.

Of course, there are no guarantees that a fall won't happen, but awareness of possibilities and alertness to old habits that might cause problems at this stage of our lives could stave off a fall. I had a very active, independent eighty-year-old aunt who had a long set of basement stairs leading to her laundry room. She went up and down those stairs many times a week without a struggle. She was strong and able to manage a laundry basket and stairs with no problem. She just had one bad habit: She wore scuff-style bedroom slippers. In the beginning of her eightieth decade, she fell down those steps she had climbed so often and so easily. Unfortunately, she never recovered. Within a few days of her fall, she was gone.

Lack of sleep

Sleep often becomes an issue as we age. Hormones that kept us sleepy and attached to the bed when we were younger no longer flow through our bodies the way they used to. Insomnia often sneaks in, and we face feeling irritable, dragging around during the day, and fearing the onset of bedtime. That then drives us to seek all sorts of solutions, including what seems like tried-and-true over-the-counter cure-alls. Maybe you've been there.

Resorting to over-the-counter sleep aids seems to be a common way to help the sleepless sleep, and yet Dr. Friesen warned me a long time ago, "Stay away from those!" Acetaminophen and diphenhydramine, the two products in these kinds of medicine, seem harmless, but health risks have been linked to regular use. Acetaminophen is linked to kidney disease, a fact now recognized by the FDA.[1] One study indicated that the long-term use of nonaspirin, nonsteroidal anti-inflammation drugs and acetamino- phen products might increase the risk of kidney cancer.[2] Then there's diphenhydramine, which brings the sleep-aid component to the medicine. It falls into the class of medi- cines known as anticholinergics. (By the way, remember *anti* means "against.") Within every brain cell, a simple B vitamin—choline—is rapidly converted into acetylcholine, the major neurotransmitter responsible for memory, learn- ing, and verbal reasoning in our brains. When the cho- linergic system is ravaged by time and anticholinergic medications, dementia is one of the sad results.[3] Memories fade, personalities change, and judgment is impaired. There is no need to take something to sleep that could have long- term implications for your life. There are better choices.

The best supplements you can use to soothe your

out-of-kilter sleep patterns are tryptophan and melatonin. These both are natural supplemental ways to help your brain acclimate itself to a better rhythm. Prescription sedatives such as Xanax or Ativan steal REM ("rapid eye movement") sleep away if used nightly. These medications are so effective at impairing recall that they are routinely used prior to uncomfortable medical procedures. If you want to stay your best mental self, avoid the regular use of prescription sedatives.

The best schedule you can follow is waking up at the same time every morning. It doesn't matter when you go to bed, according to the good doctor, but waking up at the same time ensures that you will experience REM sleep. REM sleep is critical. In fact, without it, memory and learning are impaired, and then irritability and anxiety follow. Depression is most likely not far behind. Without REM sleep, creativity suffers and life loses that sense of joy that comes with fully restful and restorative sleep. Think about this: That spark of creativity you see or experience is directly related to the amount of time spent in REM sleep.

Dr. Friesen tells many of his sleep-struggling patients to enjoy their time awake when sleep eludes them. It is time to be alive, to read or listen to music. Choosing to see this "additional" time awake as an opportunity to count your blessings (literally) can become a powerful tool to help rewire and rejuvenate an aging brain. As a general rule, we require less sleep as we age.[4]

As the years roll by, another problem with sleeping is breathing. Sometimes a full-blown CPAP or BiPAP machine is the answer for diagnosed sleep apnea, but let's face it—not everyone is willing to be connected to a machine to sleep. Even if it provides the needed oxygen and gives a decent night's sleep, the thought of being hooked to a machine is abhorrent to some. An amazing step-down from being connected to the machine is a very simple over-the-counter remedy: nasal strips. Airflow through our nasal passages follows a very strict principle that is well known to physicists and physicians alike—Bernoulli's principle. Simply put, the narrower a passageway, the greater the resistance to airflow. The greater the resistance, the more our airways vibrate, creating the disturbing sound recognized as snoring. Because of Bernoulli's principle, even a tiny increase in the diameter of our nasal passages relieves snoring and restores normal, restful sleep—and nasal strips do just that. Nasal strips can also help with that annoying nighttime stuffiness that can break into your sleep. Using nasal strips can also spare you from over-the-counter nasal sprays, which have a whole story of their own, particularly sprays that contain oxymetazoline.

My friend Lynda had no idea that regularly using an oxymetazoline spray was a problem. (For the record, saline solution doesn't have the same issues as oxymetazoline.) Several years ago she began using a couple of shots in her nose before she went to sleep at night. Our little nightly routines matter more than we know! Concurrent with her usage of this nasal spray, she began experiencing strange, short episodes of spiking blood pressure. Three or four times, she lost the capacity to speak coherently for a minute or so. Naturally she was concerned and went for medical help. Despite undergoing all the latest tests, she received no conclusive results. All that turned up was elevated blood pressure. Her internist carefully monitored and medicated her to try to keep her blood pressure in check. Recently she was in her ophthalmologist's office and casually mentioned that she was using a nasal spray for her stuffiness. The lights went on! "What? You're using oxymetazoline? Well, no wonder! It causes blood pressure spikes. You need to stop immediately!" She did, and her blood pressure has been normal ever since.

When I told Lynda's story to Dr. Friesen, he said, in his typical teaching fashion, "Well, this isn't a story about oxymetazoline or about blood pressure. It's a story about full disclosure." Things that can seem very small, he told me, can be very big. Over-the-counter meds, health store supplements, or something you feel no need to mention may be the very thing that is at the root of your problem. We often have the mentality, probably instilled in us years ago, that we shouldn't bother our doctor with little details. So we don't fully disclose what we are taking. But since we don't really know what can or can't be harmful, it really is critical to go ahead and tell it all. My friend Lynda would be the first to say yes to that advice! Who would think a couple of little sprays of an over-the-counter nasal spray could so impact your life?

It may be that your desire to seem well and act younger than your years keeps you from being totally truthful with your doctor. I've seen this with some gen Xers I know, and I have seen it in myself. I have recognized that I need to dial back my desire to be okay so it doesn't cloud my true concerns when I see my doctors. I don't want to worry them or seem more decrepit than I am, so my optimistic self shows up. Maybe you're the same way. While being positive is critical to our well-being, there is a fine line between a cover-up and the truth! When it comes to our relationships with our doctors, we need to deal in truth and nothing but the truth.

One more thing for those of you who might think it's really easier to just run by the "Doc in the Box" to get your medical care: Don't forget the importance of someone who knows you. Medicine is not mechanics. You are not a car with a schematic set of directions that fits every car of a certain make and model. Seeing a different mechanic every time may work for keeping your car going, but for a human, having a health provider who gets to know you is a good thing.

Foods and inflammation
One process that causes problems in our bodies is inflammation. Our bodies are able to easily deal with acute

inflammation, such as a simple paper cut. Redness, swelling, and warmth are all manifestations of inflammation that usually disappear in a day or two as our bodies do their healing work. On the other hand, chronic, systemic, low-grade inflammation that goes on for months or years is an entirely different matter. Chronic inflammation is the final common denominator for almost any disease you can think of—Alzheimer's disease, diabetes, arthritis, obesity, high blood pressure, heart disease, and cancer, just to name a few.

Foods that we carelessly pop in our mouths can feed this inflammation without our even knowing it. Foods that contain high-fructose corn syrup (HFCS) are among the worst. Check it out: crackers, ketchup, candy? You'll find it. Whipped cream in an aerosol can? It's there. Boxed foods, canned foods, fast foods, low-fat foods, and foods you would never believe are tainted with this potent, addictive ingredient. Carbonated beverages are culprits too. Most bottles contain fifteen teaspoons of "sugar," and virtually all of it is in the form of high-fructose corn syrup. This would not represent a health hazard if HFCS were consumed in tiny doses; however, Americans have gone from consuming two pounds of sugar a year two hundred years ago to consuming a whopping one hundred and fifty-two pounds per year.[5] To quote Paracelsus, a Swiss physician from the sixteenth century, "The dose makes the poison."

With so many processed foods containing HFCS, the potential for health problems rises exponentially, including problems associated with leftover mercury that is found in our soda drinks.[6] Why do manufacturers use HFCS instead of simple cane sugar, you ask? Well, corn is cheap compared to cane sugar. There is a long scientific explanation for why you should avoid HFCS (you can find it in the literature if you're so inclined),[7] but the bottom line is that it interacts with the inflammation process in your body to create more inflammation. It's an ugly cycle that can be hard to halt.

While we're all aware of our cholesterol numbers, few of us know about or ever mention our inflammation numbers. The medical field is coming to the conclusion now that the inflammation in our bodies can be of greater concern than our cholesterol. For example, having both inflammation and high cholesterol equals high potential of heart disease. Having high cholesterol and no inflammation, by contrast, means that the potential for heart disease is exceedingly low. You can ask your medical provider about a test for inflammation (a C-reactive protein, or CRP, blood test) during your annual exam. We need to learn how to be as preventative as possible when it comes to inflammation.

We can implement the most preventative measures in our diet, and it's not hard! That's the great thing. No matter what age you are or what season you are in, you can do so much for yourself when you decide to eat well. Here are some high points to remember:

> Always eat breakfast and don't eat after 6:30 p.m.

> Avoid trans fats. Read labels. A lot of restaurants have eliminated trans fats. Become a trans-fat detective, and you'll be amazed at both what you can avoid and what you can eat without concern. Be knowledgeable. Pay attention. You don't have to become a "food pain," but just quietly be mindful of what you're eating!

> Don't overdo it on dairy products.

> Include as much Mediterranean cuisine in your diet as possible:

   Eat lamb, fish, chicken, and beef or venison.
   Eat organic eggs, which have lots of omega-3 in them.
   Use cold-pressed, extra-virgin olive oil and organic coconut oil.
   Eat unprocessed nuts and nut butters.
   Eat brown or wild rice.
   Eat multigrain bread. Genesis and Ezekiel bread both are winners.
   Eat vegetables with lots of color. Bright-colored fruits and vegetables will do the work for you.

> Embrace antioxidants. Fruits and vegetables can be a great source of antioxidants such as polyphenols and resveratrol. Antioxidants will give you the "so much more" of what your body requires to be healthy. Your body, skin, and hair really will thank you!

> Don't take calcium. According to a recent study from Johns Hopkins, "taking calcium in the form of supplements may raise the risk of plaque buildup in arteries and heart damage." This is particularly true for women. So lay off the calcium supplements and take your vitamin D_3. Our bodies are wonderfully made. If you take 5,000 to 10,000 milligrams of vitamin D_3 every day, your body will absorb the calcium it needs, and you won't have to deal with the downside of supplements.[8]

> Make fish oil (ultrapurified and microfiltered omega-3) your best friend. If you have trouble taking fish oil capsules because of the burp factor, keep them in the freezer and take them at night. You'll be amazed. You won't even know you've taken them. (Be sure you don't buy fish oil with omega-6. It will lead to the dreaded inflammation we're trying so hard to avoid! Remember, it's all about paying attention.)

> Drink lots of water! Eight eight-ounce glasses a day is ideal, but the point is to drink as much as you

can. I have a cup that I keep with me all the time.
I keep it filled with ice and filtered water and often
a shot of lemon. It makes me happy and makes me
want to drink water. In fact, that's all I drink. I've
been weaned from everything else. I don't even like
the flavor of the sodas and flavored drinks I used to
enjoy!

While food is what we use to handle most inflammation issues, there are a few things besides food to consider.
There are a couple of daily reminders we all need: Brush
and floss at least twice a day! Flossing is so important as
we get older. The "food junk" that gathers around the base
of our teeth is nothing but a bacteria-producing mine-
field. One reason flossing is so important is that your heart
doesn't take kindly to inflammatory problems in your
mouth—or any other place in your body, for that matter.
A brushed and flossed mouth is a healthy mouth.

Now if you are really interested in a fun thing to do that
will clean your mouth in addition to brushing and flossing, try "pulling." Pulling is a funky, fun exercise where
you put a teaspoon of coconut oil in your mouth and swish
it around for twenty minutes. (The time seems important.) Then you spit it out in a trash can. (Don't spit in
your drain—it will clog it up, especially if you have a septic
tank.) Why would you do this? Well, it's been around for
a couple of thousand years, and those who do it swear by

it! It cleans the bacteria out of your mouth, brightens up your teeth, and is just good for you!

Now I get it—you may not be this adventuresome, and if that's the case, no judgment here! The main thing is to take care of your teeth as much as possible. Brush, floss, brush, floss, and you'll have developed a habit that will keep your mouth healthy. If you avoid inflammation and infection in your mouth, your whole body will be better off.

Brain matters

I just took one of those ten-minute walk breaks we need to take when we've been sitting. (Believe me, writing a book will give you every reason to sit!) But I'm back to write about one more thing I almost forgot. You're not going to believe what I "almost forgot": Yep, it's your brain! The brain is the most important organ in our bodies. If your brain doesn't work, then it won't matter whether you can stand up from a sitting position or your heart is pumping well. The brain is the control center of the whole body, and as we go through each season, there are things we can do to keep our brains healthy.

I've already mentioned some medications to avoid, some foods to embrace, and the little habits that keep us going, but this is just as critical: Be careful what you think! If you meditate on what's wrong, what you've lost, what you are deficient in, and how awful things are in this world, your brain is going to suffer. No matter how well you feed it and relax it, it just doesn't do well if you are bound up with worry, bitterness, and anxiety. The main thing to do is to be good to your brain. You will want it functioning well as it goes with you toward ninety. Trust me—you won't want to get there without it. There are diseases and deficiencies that we can't stave off, but we can keep our minds as sharp as they can be. Read, stay curious, forgive, drop the bitterness, and pursue peace. Sounds like a simple formula, but if you can remember to do these things, you'll be ahead of the game no matter what your age.

The psalmist speaks of the person who has lived well and maintained his reason for living. It all works together. I want to do what I can to head toward ninety with the grace of one who flourishes and yields fruit in old age. Don't you? Read these words and let them sink into your heart. There's just something about the Psalms that soothes and encourages the soul. Psalm 92 begins with "It is good to give thanks to the LORD and to sing praises to Your name, O Most High; to declare Your lovingkindness in the morning and Your faithfulness by night." Any time there's a declaration in the Scriptures that something is "good," you can know a wealth of spiritual health is waiting when you do it. If you start the day declaring His lovingkindness and close the day declaring His faithfulness, what a difference it can make in your outlook, whether you are heading toward thirty, sixty, or ninety! Read some more of this very rich psalm and meditate on what it says:

> The righteous man will flourish like the palm tree,
> He will grow like a cedar in Lebanon.
> Planted in the house of the LORD,
> They will flourish in the courts of our God.
> They will still yield fruit in old age;
> They shall be full of sap and very green,
> To declare that the LORD is upright;
> *He is* my rock, and there is no unrighteousness in
>   Him.

PSALM 92:12-15

At every stage of life, we have a purpose. And no matter your age, from millennial to boomer and beyond, if you're going to live, you might as well live as well as possible to fulfill the purpose for which you were made. A little change in food and drink, a little movement modification, and some checks against "stinking thinking" can make the road to ninety so much smoother.

It's said that when a man named Eubie Blake reached the age of one hundred, he spoke that famous line, "If I'd known I was going to live this long, I'd have taken better care of myself." May we all remember Eubie's lament and take care of ourselves before we zoom past that ninety we were shooting for!

CHAPTER EIGHT

WHAT ABOUT THE CHILDREN?

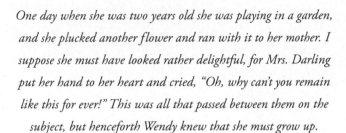

One day when she was two years old she was playing in a garden, and she plucked another flower and ran with it to her mother. I suppose she must have looked rather delightful, for Mrs. Darling put her hand to her heart and cried, "Oh, why can't you remain like this for ever!" This was all that passed between them on the subject, but henceforth Wendy knew that she must grow up.

J. M. BARRIE, *PETER PAN*

WHO DOES NOT REMEMBER the plaintive chords of "Sunrise, Sunset"?

Is this the little girl I carried?
Is this the little boy at play?

I don't remember growing older—
When did they?

If you're of the boomer generation, you first heard this touching song in the wedding scene from *Fiddler on the Roof*. If you're a gen Xer or a millennial, you may have first heard it in the scratchy duet between Timon and Pumbaa in *The Lion King* as they wonder how Simba has grown so much in so little time. It's a question adults always seem to have about children: How did they grow up and we're still the same? Things are constantly changing while we're living the same life day to day. Children becoming adults is a hard concept with which adults have to grapple.

Not that long ago, our children were little and we were in charge. Now they're grown, and we're not in charge anymore. We've been the adults their whole lives, and now they are adults too. It seems like that would make things easier, but those roles we've played for so many years as parents and children have a way of affecting feelings and perceptions, and sometimes they can create a bit of tension. Although we're all adults now, the parent-child relationship remains. It usually is very different, but we are still parents, and they are still our children.

I often laugh when I think about aging parents asking one another, "What are we going to do about the children?" while their adult children are asking one another, "What are we going to do about Mom and Dad?" Those thoughts and conversations make our winter-season relationships so rich and yet sometimes so complex.

It is a hard thing to face the facts of life. Fact: There will come a time for each of us, if it has not already come, when we will not be the strong ones. We on whom all decisions used to rest will make fewer and fewer decisions.

Another fact: Adult children do not like to see changes in their aging parents. Those who have always been there are no longer the dependable presence they once were. The winds of change are steady, always hinting of transitions to come. If there is one thing the years have taught us, it's that with any change there will be adjustment.

I've heard it said that the first ten years of parenting go by slowly, then the next ten years fly by in a flash. There's another truth to which I can attest as well: After the twentieth year, life becomes a blur. Graduations, marriages, children, jobs, moves, deployments, illnesses, divorces, grandchildren, grandparents' illnesses, deaths, funerals, family gatherings, family decisions, hurts, gratitude, joys, and pain all make up the years after the children leave home. The decades move by hardly noticed, and the children become adults facing their own midlife issues. How did it happen? How can it be? Somehow, before we notice, we all will find ourselves living in the last quarter of our own lives.

If you're a parent, I'm sure if you stopped for a moment you could fill a page describing your relationship with your growing, changing children. Given time, you could fill many pages with your feelings about these days of your life—and yet, who has the time? It's all happened so fast.

In this twenty- to thirty-year process of watching children grow, you will probably see some fairly dramatic changes in yourself. If you're not there already, you'll soon be facing the predictable changes of aching joints, slacking energy, sleepless nights, and graying hair (or the standing appointments with your hairstylist to cover that gray hair!). That's all to be expected. We'll laugh about those things among our friends. It's easy to be self-deprecating with those who are going through the same thing. Sometimes, though, we end up facing situations we never dreamed we'd face, and we're surprised to find ourselves looking for a place to land on issues with our adult children. Those are challenges we may not be so quick to share, and yet the process of dealing with children at this stage can seem as interminable as those first ten labor-intensive years of their lives.

Many of us approach the unknown seasons of being parents of adult children, or adult children of aging parents, with trepidation. We haven't known each other in these ways before. But take courage: These are paths many have walked and thrived in, and there are things both parents and children can do to navigate these seasons well. Following are some guidelines that can give you more insight in the midst of your dealings with one another.

Being the Aging Parent of an Adult Child
If your children follow the prescribed path for growing up and leaving home, and your relationship is fairly uncomplicated,

then be grateful and thank God for the gift of easy transitions. They are possible, and perhaps this is what happens in the majority of families (although I haven't seen any statistics!). Some children were just born to cooperate. For other parent-children teams, the transition may not be so easy. Many experiences and quirks can factor into bumpy transitions, but some basic rules will help smooth out the road and keep it smoother in the future.

Recognize that the rules have changed.

When your adult children are not living under your roof and are not dependent on your financial support, you no longer call the shots for them. I've found that many adult children feel unspoken pressure to do what their parents expect, even when the parents haven't said how they feel about a particular issue. Sometimes it's important to say up-front, "I don't expect you to _____" if there is anything you think they may be doing or not doing because it would make you unhappy. Truth is, your expectations may be good, but the season has come to allow them to fully function as the adults they are. Letting go of your need to have things done your way can make everyone happier.

The next rule for the season may seem redundant, but it is oh so important to remember.

Remember they're adults.

Since the children are now adults, we don't have the right to blurt out whatever is on our minds. As we grow older, it's easier to say what we think and consider it a "right," but we can make comments that would be better left unsaid to those who have grown up with us. What we would never say to a girlfriend should hold true for our children. We probably wouldn't say to our best bud, "Wow, it looks like you've put on weight." Nor would we mention the zit on her face, the condition of her shoes, or anything that would make her feel like an "epic fail." Yet the parents of adult children sometimes feel they retain the right to say what they please because they are the parents. After all, the children will always be "the children"! Respect in the way you communicate to your children is a gift for which they will bless you—maybe after you're gone, but ultimately they will appreciate it.

And just so you don't feel as if you have abdicated every parental role you have, the next rule of smooth transitions is for you!

It's your roof and your rules.

You can't make your adult children believe or do anything they don't want to believe or do, but if your values are truly based on your deeply held convictions, then don't let your adult children run over you or your values while they are under your roof.

If you have convictions about your unmarried children sleeping with their significant other, then don't make provision for them to do so under your roof. This is where it takes grace and a lot of love to stick to your guns. In the long run, you and your children will both have more respect for one another if you kindly abide by the same convictions you've had all along. This may seem old fashioned and a little behind the times, but being who you are at the core is important. They know how you feel, so don't compromise just because it's easier to give in.

Love and acceptance should never be the issue. Love your child and accept him or her with open arms. Extend that acceptance to whomever your child brings to your home. If they insist on sleeping together, however, you just don't have a place for them. If it becomes an issue, it's not a matter of their sleeping together. It's a matter of what is respectful to your wishes in your house. If your child accepts sleeping on the couch in the basement and the friend takes the little bedroom upstairs, then of course they're welcome to stay with you. Clearly, no matter how involved they are, they can spend a couple of nights apart out of respect for the rules of the house. If they balk at the thought, then their insistence on being together is more about proving a point than about disappointment that Mom and Dad don't accept their freethinking ways. So let them spring for a hotel and see them for breakfast in the morning.

The same is true for alcohol, drugs, or anything else you feel doesn't fit into your value system. Your kids know you and know what you believe, so you do no one any favors by being silent or caving in to their wishes just to prove that you're the all-accepting parent. Be who you are, filled with love and kindness, and let the chips fall where they may.

Just a hint for those who are the parents of teenagers: If you insist on certain rules of the house now, it's likely there won't be as many questions about it when your children come home as adults. They will just know that "My mom and dad won't go for this." Serve the best cookies in the neighborhood and remain true to your values. It's a great combination, and the principle will hold true whether they are fifteen or forty-five.

Now don't forget: When you go to visit your adult children, it's *their* roof and *their* rules. Don't get that mixed up. You only can rule under your own roof, but you can always take your award-winning cookies when you visit!

Leave the changing to God.

One of the greatest complaints of adult children, among those who have complaints, is the lament, "My parents don't miss an opportunity to preach to me." Many a potentially good relationship has been ruined by the parent who couldn't leave the preaching to the pastor and the changing to God. Often parents feel so invested in the outcome of their adult child's behavior that they can't relax and let God do business with their child.

One of the loveliest women I know has spent a lifetime trying to be okay with her mother. No matter what she does, she gets a sermon in response. Consequently, there is no relationship. This is not what either the mother or the daughter wants, but there is always a sermon standing between them and their potentially loving relationship. It's as if the mom believes that if she doesn't preach, her daughter is bound for the wrath of God. What she doesn't realize is that her daughter knows the mistakes she's made; she is hearing straight from God through her own search of the Scriptures and communion with Him. There's just too much history for her to hear it from her mother. It's her mom's job to love her and to trust God with the rest—an old adage that has been true for mothers since the days of the Old Testament.

Jochebed was the mother of baby Moses at a time when Pharaoh was on a rampage to kill all the Jewish baby boys in the land of Egypt. She was able to protect him for three months, but like all babies, he became noisy, and she had to find a way to hide him from Pharaoh's soldiers. So she wove a little basket and waterproofed it with tar and pitch. Knowing she had to trust God with her tiny boy, she wrapped him in a little blanket, lovingly placed him in the basket, and put him in the bulrushes by the Nile. I believe she was emotionally unable to watch, so she sent his older sister to watch and see what happened to him.

Of course, we know the familiar story. Pharaoh's daughter and her maids came down to the river and spotted the basket. When the princess opened the basket, little

Moses cried and Pharaoh's daughter had compassion on him. She recognized him as one of the Hebrew baby boys who were under her father's death edict. When Moses was discovered, his sister stepped up and asked if the princess wanted a Hebrew woman to nurse the baby. So Moses was returned to his biological mother until he was weaned. She knew she would have to give him up again, but for that moment, she had her baby back. In that story of a mother's love bound up with impossible circumstances, I believe we see the mother's motto for all time: Do what you can do and trust God with the rest.

No matter how old your children are or how old you are, it is inherent in your mother-heart to do something when your child is in trouble. You want to change your child or his or her circumstances. So do what you can, but don't forget to trust God with the rest! Too often we forget that part. We do what we can do (and too often it is preaching), but we fail to trust God with the outcome.

Be a source of joy to your adult children.

Sometimes in the winter season of our lives, we spend so much time focusing on what hurts or is hard that we forget to have fun (or be fun), and our adult children don't enjoy being around us.

My aunt Jane is ninety. She is one of those people who has always found fun in living. The first picture I ever saw of her was a professional photo with her siblings. It was one of those old everybody-has-to-be-serious photographs, and truly the children were. Like stair steps, starting with the oldest (my mother), five of the six children stood at attention with serious faces. My aunt Jane was two at the time. Her twin, Jean, stood dutifully by her, being a proper child, but Jane could not hold it in. She was having fun holding her dress out and posing with an irrepressible smile. She just had to have fun! For all her life, Jane has been a favorite in the family because she has always wanted everyone around her to have fun. At a recent reunion where we celebrated her ninetieth birthday, the cousins all reminisced about time spent at Aunt Jane's. Everyone had the same memory: "She let us do what we wanted to do and have fun." That is her legacy. If you are around her, she's looking for the joy in the moment, and she invites you to share it with her.

You may not be wired for merrymaking, but knowing what people like and making sure you provide it when they are around is a wonderful legacy to leave.

What are your people's favorite foods? Do you know? My teenage grandson, Luke, loves my fried okra. I try to include it in every meal he has with us because I know it makes him happy. (By the way, it's not just any fried okra. It is a particular store brand that is lightly battered, and I fry it in coconut oil. I know, I know, but that's the way he likes it! Nothing else will do, and as long as I am around to cook it, I hope he will come around and eat it!)

Joy doesn't just flow one way in generational relationships that work well. There is a reciprocal delight that can
be found as adult children begin to recognize things they
can do that will bring blessing to their older parents. This
takes a certain level of maturity that some never attain,
but for those who do, there is blessing upon blessing to
be received.

Being the Adult Child of an Aging Parent

I love the story of Julia and Claire, two friends who were
having lunch. Both were retired professionals who were
fully proficient in sharing pictures from their iPhones.
Claire asked Julia about her daughter who had moved
back to the East Coast from Chicago: "'It must be nice to
see her more often.' Julia sighed. 'Yes, but . . . Whenever
[she] drops by, I'm not sure whether she's come to visit or
to check up on me: Does my home meet the clean test? Is
the yogurt in my refrigerator long past its "use by" date?
. . . I feel like I'm constantly being assessed.'"[1]

I had to laugh when I read this little scenario. Since
my granddaughter helped me clean out my cupboards (per
my request) and discovered some cans that were "severely"
outdated, I have been much more aware of what such neg-
ligence means to those who are younger. She laughingly
said, "Gan Gan, this stuff has to go." I thought, *Uh-oh, I've
become that person. They're going to have to keep an eye on me!*
So she threw the cans away, and I've been on my best "use

by" behavior ever since. The day may be coming, however, when I won't be able to stay on top of things like that. With enough years, the things that mattered at one time seem to slip away. Sharpness can go, and we may be left trying to act like our old selves even when things have clearly changed.

I think no one realizes what the feeling of not being quite yourself is like until you're there. I look back at the things I was impatient with in my aging parents and wish I had been wiser and more aware about how it feels to have slipped into winter's coldest days. I guess you can't know until you know, but hopefully if you have aging parents and are reading this, you will be more aware than I was.

My mother lived to the eve of her ninetieth year. Her hearing loss was a problem for many years prior to her death. We talked about it often, and I encouraged her to do something about her hearing. She did what she could, but she found the hearing aids of those days to be cumbersome, annoying, and "no help at all." After she died, we found two brand-new sets of hearing aids in her dresser drawer. She hated how they made her feel, so she refused to wear them. I have to admit that I had a low-grade annoyance with her for not being able to hear and not being willing to wear the hearing aids. Her need for everything to be repeated cut short some conversations that I would cherish now. Ten years after she's gone, however, I'd love to repeat anything she wanted me to repeat as loudly as she needed me to say it. But we don't get do-overs, do we?

Be as patient as possible.

From years of experience I'd tell you that if you are an adult child dealing with aging parents, your parents really want your patience. If they could, they would act like the parents you remember. They would still have their hearing, their memory, their sense of boundaries, and their tidiness. No one wants to be the oldest one in the room because there are so many stereotypes (and obvious truths) associated with being old. To have your adult children roll their eyes and jokingly reference what you're lacking is a painful thing to experience. Despite the banter that goes along with being old, there's a fine line of self-doubt that comes with it. You may joke about age, but you can bet that as your parents get older and find familiar activities difficult, they will love your understanding. It all boils down to seeking to understand *as much as* seeking to be understood! It's true for both sides of the equation. Patience and understanding, although never easy, go miles toward making good relationships.

Free your parents from solving your problems.

Despite the fact your parents are always your parents, as they age they have less capacity to emotionally handle your problems. You may have depended on their wisdom and support as you were growing up, but at some point they will no longer be able to provide a shoulder for you to lean on. There is something about aging that weakens the capacity for "bearing burdens." This is when everyone in the family needs to be a grown-up. While carrying your own burdens and keeping them off your parents isn't always easy to accomplish, it's a worthy goal.

Often during this time, how to relate to parents becomes a source of tension for siblings. The more responsible one is irritated with the less responsible one. The one who has leaned on Mom or Dad for the most help can be resentful when a sibling steps in and says "No more." Unfortunately, the dysfunction of the early years doesn't get any better in the later years. When parents age, however, children need to be intentional to focus on Mom and Dad. Spare your parents the pain of how you feel about your siblings. You may never come to terms with your brothers and sisters, but protecting your parents from the conflict is one small gift you can give them before they are gone.

Respect the position of parent.
Parents and children have a relationship that resembles the balancing act between the two sides of an old-fashioned scale. Over the years, the scales change. The parents, who were the heavyweights, become the lightweights, and the children, who were the lightweights, become the heavyweights. The decision makers change places. Sometimes this can cause angst because as age advances and parents become the lightweights, they still are entitled to make

decisions about their own lives. This is not the time for children to think, *Well, I need to parent my parents.* That time may come, but as long as parents can make their own decisions, they need to be allowed to do so.

Courtland Milloy wrote a column for the *Washington Post* describing his experience as a long-distance caregiver. His parents lived in Louisiana, and he wanted to do the best for them. He had understood from "some elder-care experts" that "when aging parents stop acting in their own best interest, the grown children must 'reverse roles' and simply make them do the right thing."[2]

Milloy soon discovered that this perspective was wrong. As he pondered what to do about his parents, he asked himself what the right thing was to do. He was asking the question for himself and for so many children of aging parents. Everybody wants to do the right thing, but what is it? When do you intervene? As long as your parent is not hurting himself or others, what is the right thing to do?

Another columnist, reflecting on aging parents, wrote, "A wise man once said it like this: 'When I was 22, I did some things my parents thought were remarkably stupid. But I was an adult and they were my choices. Now, my parents may be doing some things that I think are remarkably stupid. But they have the same right to make mistakes as I did.'"[3]

Respect for your aging parents' right to make decisions

for as long as possible is another gift with which you can grace them. Taking their thoughts and desires into consideration may make more work for you, but it will give your parents a sense of maintaining independence and respect.

That is the basis for the fifth commandment: "Honor your father and your mother, that your days may be prolonged in the land" (Exodus 20:12). The word *honor* means "'to give weight to someone.'"[4] I like to think of honoring aging parents as giving weight to them by respecting their choices and decisions despite their frailty and the fact they have become the lightweights.

Granted, the day may come—whether due to dementia or to some other mental decline—when your parents no longer are able to make safe decisions for themselves. At that point, even though you love and respect them and want to "give weight" to who they are, you may have to make the really hard decisions for them, even if they don't agree with you. There will be grace for those days, but being in that place is difficult.

Bob Deffinbaugh addressed the words from Exodus 20:12:

> Honoring our parents is one of the highest
> callings and the greatest tasks we face in life.
> There are two great tasks in life to which most of
> us are called. The first is the bearing and raising
> of children, to bring them from the absolute

dependence of the womb, to the independence of adolescence, to the maturity of adulthood. The second is the caring for our own parents in their declining years. Often this involves the deterioration of the physical body, and frequently of the mind. The raising of children has its pains, but it usually is accompanied by the joy of seeing our children grow up, become mature and responsible, and independent. The caring for our parents is seldom as rewarding. The culmination of this process is the grave.[5]

And so with these words we close the chapter, although the discussion never ends and the unknown seasons keep coming. The experiences of being a parent to a child and a child to a parent are among the most complicated, tender, tough, transcendent relationships any of us will ever know, and the seasonal changes that come with them can be challenging. When a family is created, that parent-child bond is formed, and we never fully escape the connection, no matter how long or difficult. As we were cared for when we came into the family as helpless infants, so we care for those who cared for us as they become more helpless. We didn't know they were caring for us when we were infants, and they may reach the point where they don't know we're caring for them. The knowing doesn't matter. The job needs to be done. Whether you are the parent or the child or both, you will work it out. It's an unavoidable and unknown season for parents and children. The experience will always be part of who you are, who you've been, and who you are becoming. I think it's meant to be that way.

CHAPTER NINE

CLEAN UP AFTER YOURSELF

❦

Out of clutter, find simplicity; from discord, find
harmony; in the middle of difficulty lies opportunity.

ALBERT EINSTEIN

THE REALIZATION THAT IT'S TIME for us or someone we love to go to a safer place to live brings a lot of upheaval and questioning. First, just the idea of having to move from the familiar to the unfamiliar is unnerving. Then there are the interminable details. The fact that we have to talk about moving when it can be so emotional is even more unsettling. It would be so much easier if it would just happen without having to face all the feelings from everyone involved. Whether you are the one being faced with a move from all you've found familiar or the one who has to move people you love from their home of many years, you're going to deal with inner angst.

Talking about such a move with grace can be daunting. The conversation may go well, and it may not. But the reality is, someone is going to have to clean up the things being left behind. No one leaves this earth without leaving a bit of clutter. We all just need to decide how much we'll leave and, in kindness, choose what to do with it without putting that burden on others. It's a new and very unknown season for everyone involved. If you are the older person, you're giving things up. If you're the younger person, you're trying to figure out what to do with the things the older one is leaving.

It can be confusing, gut-wrenching, and just plain painful to be faced with what the old folks used to call "breaking up housekeeping." That's an antiquated term that means you don't function in your role as "keeper of the home" anymore. It means your stuff will be dispersed and you're probably going to live somewhere besides the home you've loved or at least found familiar.

In this kind of transition, every generation is affected, and usually each has to be involved in the new arrangement. If you are the one who has to move, "breaking up housekeeping" means you have to decide what you're going to do with a lifetime of collected things. The more clarity you can have about this, the better, because it's *your* stuff being dispersed, sold, or stored. This can be very emotional and confusing unless you've prepared yourself ahead of time with a healthy dose of reality. The stuff has to be dealt with, and someone has to do it! Many of us wait too long, thinking the next generation will want what we've collected, only to find out they really are not interested in our stuff. It's more of a burden than a blessing. Then what?

Life has its strange twists and turns. We spend so many years collecting furniture, knick-knacks, and memorabilia. It all seems so important to our sense of security. But then life puts on the brakes, and we have to begin getting rid of the things we thought we had to have. Of course, there will be a few (very few) things that our children and grandchildren may want as mementos of our lives, but when it comes to the sofas, end tables, and doilies that we inherited from our parents, be assured that our kids (and for sure our grandkids) want no part of them now that IKEA is on the scene. Furniture is cheap, as are most household items. Styles are changing more quickly than the weather, so your grandmother's Queen Anne sofa you had re-covered for your children to use in their home someday is basically a dinosaur that they would prefer to not feed and house. (Of course, if they happen to be rare birds who collect antiques and are attached to everything they grew up with, then forget what I just said. You've got it made. *Their* kids will no doubt have to deal with their junk. Rare birds don't usually run through too many generations!)

This responsibility of stewarding family stuff is like every other process we go through as we move from season to season. It's all about attitude. Some situations are more complicated and labor intensive than others, but having the right attitude can have a huge impact. Whether you are the one "cleaning up after yourself" or the one cleaning up after your parents or another relative, choosing a decent attitude will help you go through it with as little pain as possible. (And remember, if you get a bad attitude, it's going to do a number on your bones. Hardly worth brittle bones, is it?)

Dealing with Your Own Stuff

If you are the one making your own decision to downsize, good for you. It's really a hard decision, but in the long run, it's the kindest thing you can do for your family. There are a few things to remember that will help you as you begin the process. Of course it depends on your physical ability, but if you can, do as much yourself as possible.

Start now!

The more you can start getting rid of while you can, the happier you will be when you actually move to a smaller space. Now I realize that's making an assumption that you'll move. Most people want to "age in place," so if it's possible to maintain your home, then do it. But even if you stay in your home, decluttering—getting rid of things you'll never use again—is a kindness to yourself and to those who will come after you. Realistically, we all know that if we live long enough, we will need to make adjustments. Even if you age in place, the best thing you can do is to start cleaning up now.

Look around!

If you are in a room in your house while you're reading this, look around. What's sitting around occupying space? What can you see from where you're sitting that could easily be given away or discarded? We don't realize how much we bring in and set down in our homes. Everything we've accumulated takes up space we don't even notice until we begin looking for it, at which point our problem quickly becomes obvious.

One of the biggest space hogs is that exercise equipment you never use. Be honest: How often do you hop up on the treadmill or pull the stretchy machine out from under the bed or go out in your garage and use the barbells? Calling someone to come get the exercise equipment is a great place to begin.

Another place you'll want to spend some time is with your photographs. Since you probably didn't grow up in the digital age, your pictures may be in boxes with the promise that you're going to go through them someday. Start there and work through them. If you don't, they very well could be totally discarded with your other stuff later on. No one will have the heart for and insight into those pictures that you do. The kindest thing you can do is to discard the nonessential or the uninteresting and label and store the rest. Better still, enlist the youngsters in the family to digitally store those pictures for you. That's a good summer job for a middle schooler.

Be ruthless!

This is such a test of your ability to let stuff go versus holding on to treasures! How much stuff do you have that has no monetary or sentimental value? It's just stuff you've hung on to because you bought it or because someone (you can't remember who) gave it to you. If you'll be ruthless with the things you know you won't miss, it will be easier to be tough about the things you will miss but won't have room for.

Be generous!

We all have stuff sitting around our houses that someone else could use and love. How about the Christmas decorations you'll never use again? What about the tablecloths and napkins your kids don't want but someone else would? What about the extra sets of sheets and blankets you've collected over the years? Are they still good? You don't ever use them, but they are in the linen closet just in case. All these things could be tenderly loved and used again by people who need them.

You may even have things in storage that you're paying to keep safe, and yet you know you won't ever use them. I found myself in that dilemma after my mother passed away. We had culled and given away her things where they would be appreciated, but we ended up with an antique bedroom suite that no one in the family wanted or had room for. It had a lot of sentimental value, so I decided to keep it, as well as a few other things, in a storage unit for which I paid a hundred dollars a month. After a year, and twelve hundred dollars gone, I asked myself, *Why am I doing this? I'm paying to hang on to something that no one in the family wants and for which I have no place!* So I contacted the church missions committee that always had furniture needs. They came, picked up the bedroom suite and the few other things that were in that unit, and immediately put them to good use. I have no idea where the furniture is today, but I know someone owns a nice bedroom suite they wouldn't have if I hadn't let go of it. (And besides that, I'm a hundred dollars richer every month!)

Are you holding on to things for sentimental value? Are you thinking, *If I just hold on to this, I know someone will want it!* Ask around, and if someone does want it, they need to take it now. If everyone's been asked and no one says yes, then their "sentimental register" is not as high as yours. It's time to stop thinking about it and let it go.

Leaving stuff to people who don't want it just because

you want them to have it does them no favors. The goal is to clean up after yourself before you go, and even if you feel great and believe you'll live forever, it's always good to plan for "just in case." Remember that someone, someday will have to deal with your stuff, and they'll thank you for thinking about what you were going to do with it.

Helping Others Deal with Their Stuff

If you are the one who has to help a parent or loved one go through purging, there are some things that will help along the way. Remember that attitude issue? No one loves the job of deconstructing someone's life collection, but even though it's tough, it has to be done. In the long run, blessed are those who deal with the stuff!

When you're helping a loved one downsize, remember that you're not just dealing with their things; you're dealing with your loved one's very personality. Now, the truth is that a lot of people have no emotional investment in things. Their emotions may be tied up in their dog, an old cat, or their neighborhood. But others really *are* emotionally attached to their physical things. They have memories connected to so much of it.

I can look around my office even as I write this and see items that would mean nothing to anyone else, but I have precious memories attached to each thing I see. There's the pillow made by one of my daughters-in-law. On the front is a picture of my grandchildren all wearing mustaches. Precious to anyone but me? Perhaps not—you see, for me, there is a memory attached! There's the cup I took communion with in Israel, the pictures of my three sons in their football uniforms, and sheep bookends Kay Arthur gave me to remind me that we are shepherds of the souls God has given us. Memories are attached to everything. Do I want to let any of these things go? No, not really—but I do have a realistic view of their future value to my family. That's such an important factor to remember. Value to you does not mean value to those you love.

If you are the one who has been tasked with helping your parents downsize or move from a place they have loved, there are a few special thoughts for you to hang on to and remember.

Talk about it, talk about it, talk about it.

Failure to communicate is a guarantee of hurt feelings and squabbling. Sometimes when we fail to communicate, it's because we think something should already be understood. Why would you have to say anything else? They know how you feel. You know how they feel. So let's just get on with it. But how many of us have gotten in trouble over the years because we thought someone could read our minds or we thought we had said what we were thinking? It never hurts to repeat a thought, even if we think we've already said it. Sometimes, talking about a touchy situation several times helps the one who's having difficulty get used to the idea, and it clarifies the situation in your own head.

Don't try to force it.

Don't force your aging parents or family members to do anything against their will. You will only provoke them to dig their heels in even deeper. If you see the conversation isn't going in a productive direction, change the subject, take a break, and give your loved ones time to consider it. Sometimes they just have to think the whole thing through several times in order to be able to accept it, and sometimes you have to say it in many different ways for them to come to grips with it.

Let things get worse if they have to.

Often things have to get worse before they get better. There are natural consequences that will happen if your parents are stubborn and won't make a move toward letting things go or moving to smaller quarters where they can be cared for. Sometimes the proverbial fat has to hit the fire before anything can be done. Your parents are still your parents, and until they absolutely cannot take care of themselves, there really isn't anything you can do to make their situation better. So keep a watchful eye until the situation can't be managed as is. I know that sounds a little reckless, but remember that you can't force people to do something against their will unless they truly are incompetent and you involve the law. You only want to go there if it becomes a huge crisis.

If things are difficult, consider hiring a senior move manager. These are professionals who are trained in working through the issues of getting aging folks moved from their long-term homes to smaller places. A third party can help navigate the difficult waters and assist seniors in moving with as little complication as possible.

I had to laugh when I read about how sometimes men think all they have to do is rent a truck and pack up Mom and Dad's stuff and move them. If only it were that easy! Senior move managers can be a huge help in times like these. They do cost, but they seem to be well worth what you pay them. If the help is there and you need it, why not contact one?[1]

Don't Leave Anything Unsaid

Cleaning up our stuff doesn't just mean material items. The stuff of relationships is even more important to pay attention to. In the later-life seasons, when the hard conversations about moving and end-of-life decisions happen, so much is complicated and full of tension. No matter our stage or season, we can lose sight of the tie that really binds us: love. With the passing years and the layers of life that intervene, it's easy to forget that parents love children and children love parents. Somewhere deep in our hearts, despite the baggage and the hurts that may have accumulated, we want to let each other know, "You are loved, and this is what I love about you."

My friend Jody Noland left her work as a corporate executive with IBM to help people "leave nothing unsaid" to the important people in their lives. Jody had a friend who was diagnosed with a brain tumor. When this friend was in the hospital, he asked his wife to bring him some paper so he could write notes to his three children. He wrote wonderful words of affirmation before dying nine months later. His daughters and son were just teenagers when he wrote the letters, but even now, as parents in their thirties, they cherish those handwritten notes on lined paper. With gracious words of love and affirmation, their dad gave a gift that would sustain them through their years.

This one story ignited a passion in Jody to give people the tools to write letters of affirmation to those they love. She realized that many would love to do it but just didn't feel adequate to try it. They thought they didn't have the words or the concepts to write a heartfelt letter of affirmation, even to the people closest to them. It seems simple, but for some it can be very hard without a little nudge or direction. Even then, some people miss the chance to give the gift that could go with their loved one throughout life.

Jody's own husband missed his chance. He was diagnosed with liver cancer and lived only a few months. Despite Jody's efforts to get him to write letters to his four children, he just couldn't do it. On the day of the funeral, Jody's stepdaughter came and sat by her side and asked if her dad had left her a letter. Jody was heartbroken to have to say, "I'm sorry, honey, but he didn't." This intensified Jody's passion for helping people not only to see the need but also to actually follow through with writing the notes. She has worked with corporations, churches, and hospice groups, including pediatric hospice groups where children write letters to their parents.[2] It's a gift that can outlive any of us, so why not give it?

Jody emphasizes that these are not letters of appreciation but rather letters of affirmation. They can be as short as one page or longer if you wish. If the writer can write at all, they should be handwritten. Of course, that's an art we're losing, but whether the letters are hand printed or handwritten in cursive, they will be cherished by anyone who receives one. Just think—how would you feel if you had such a letter from someone who loved you and is now gone?

I have pictures of a grandmother I barely remember, and oddly enough I have a little receipt that has her handwritten name on it. Apparently she paid two dollars a week at the company store for furniture that she and my grandfather bought when they were first married back in 1902. Do you think I've thrown that receipt away? Absolutely not. It was part of her. I only wish I had her words of affirmation to me, her youngest granddaughter. She died when I was nine. She knew me, but I just knew about her. A piece of paper telling me what she saw in me, and the hopes and dreams she had for my future, would be a treasure if I had it now.

Jody has put together a step-by-step guide and workshop called Leave Nothing Unsaid[3] that enables people to tap into their feelings and gives them words to describe what qualities they see in their loved ones and what hopes and dreams they have for their lives. This is not just an exercise for those who are dying, although knowing you're dying can certainly add urgency to the project. Since none of us knows when we will die, it's really a task for you to do today. When Jody started her mission, two of her friends who were in their forties died unexpectedly. Age and circumstances should not be the determining factor behind leaving nothing unsaid. The fact that you're alive and have someone to love should be reason enough.

By the way, this letter is not the place for criticism or even teasing. Some people are embarrassed to speak words of affirmation, especially to loved ones in their family, so they come through the emotional gate with a backhanded compliment or a jab intended to be affectionate. This is not the time for resorting to old family ways of communicating, even if that's always been your family's style. This is a time to write true words of affirmation that speak to the very core of the person. As Jody says,

> Most of us are well versed in our own shortcomings, and tend to focus on those much more than on what is unique or special about ourselves. Words of affirmation from those who are most special to us mean so much. Often, our loved ones see the untapped potential in us that we can't see. Or they express a belief in us that shores us up when our confidence is wavering, or we've lost a job, had a disappointing setback or gotten discouraged.[4]

Words matter. Words are important. And encouraging written words from loved ones can have a tremendous impact, often outliving the writer.

As we speak of downsizing, ridding ourselves of stuff, facing the changes that aging brings—whether we are the aging one or the one watching it happen—this is what we can do to make a difference in the process: Leave nothing unsaid.

So why not get a pen, put these ideas in front of you, and begin to write?

1. Express how you feel about your loved one.
2. Affirm your loved one's most outstanding

character qualities. Use a word picture, if possible, to illustrate.

3. Describe your hopes, prayers, and dreams for the one who will receive your letter.

But more than anything, do it today and leave nothing unsaid.

Unknown seasons bring us to places we may never have considered. If you are young—say, younger than forty-five—you probably feel as if you have plenty of time to deal with your physical and emotional stuff. And I suppose in many ways you do—but remember, we're talking about unknown seasons. The unknown is unknown. None of us knows what waits.

That's not an ominous thought; it's just a fact. The greatest time of your life may be in your future. If so, you want to be prepared to face it with an unburdened life and unfettered soul! How many people say, "Oh, I wish I could do such and such, but I have this and that to deal with," and they never fully embrace the glorious season that is waiting. Why? The season was unknown and they saw no need to prepare, to unload their stuff—or at least to keep it at a minimum so the unloading could be as handy as possible.

The unknown season that awaits those who are older is really more about those who will have to deal with the stuff after you're gone. It is a kindness, a gift, a gracious act to pay attention to the collected clutter and do something about it. It is an even greater gift to leave behind words of affirmation that will forever impact the hearts of those you love. So much better to have them say, "She left me a note that meant the world to me" than to have them say, "She left me so much stuff."

Jesus' words about stuff can leave us with the right perspective. Ponder His words and examine your own heart. Whether you're a boomer, gen Xer, or millennial, when Jesus speaks, He always touches the deepest matters of our hearts.

> Someone in the crowd said to Him, "Teacher, tell my brother to divide the family inheritance with me." But He said to him, "Man, who appointed Me a judge or arbitrator over you?" Then He said to them, "Beware, and be on your guard against every form of greed; for not even when one has an abundance does his life consist of his possessions." And He told them a parable, saying, "The land of a rich man was very productive. And he began reasoning to himself, saying, 'What shall I do, since I have no place to store my crops?' Then he said, 'This is what I will do: I will tear down my barns and build larger ones, and there I will store all my grain and my goods. And I will say to my soul, "Soul, you have many goods laid up for

many years to come; take your ease, eat, drink and be merry.'" But God said to him, 'You fool! This very night your soul is required of you; and now who will own what you have prepared?' So is the man who stores up treasure for himself, and is not rich toward God." LUKE 12:13-21

Oh, that we all would learn that in every season, we must be rich toward God!

CHAPTER TEN

GRIEF AND HOPE

———⊗≋⊗———

Grief is a journey, often perilous and without clear direction.
. . . The experience of grieving cannot be ordered or
categorized, hurried or controlled, pushed aside or ignored
indefinitely. It is inevitable as breathing, as change, as
love. It may be postponed, but it will not be denied.

MOLLY FUMIA

GRIEF IS ONE OF THOSE WORDS we all believe we understand until we are in the middle of it—and then we understand only in layers of revelation. I've come to believe that grief is what we feel when we find ourselves in the unknown seasons of life, whenever they come and whatever they may be.

Usually when we think of the word *grief*, we equate it with *sad*, but really it's so much more than that. *Grief* is hurt, anxiety, darkness, and many doubts all rolled into one word. We hear people make reference to "she's grieving" or "he is grief stricken." That usually means that person has experienced a loss and is going through emotional angst. The actual word, though, comes from the French verb *grever,* which means to "afflict, burden, oppress."[1] Grief is affliction, oppression, a burden we have to bear, but in due time it's a burden we have to lay down in order to survive.

For many, grieving is like putting together a jigsaw puzzle: You start out with a messy pile of memories and emotions. There is no linear way to go through it, and it won't follow a tightly defined plan or timetable. Putting the puzzle together requires looking at the big picture. When you first open the lid and see the jumbled mess, making sense of any of it seems impossible until you begin to take the pieces out of the box and turn them right side up. It is then that you have begun creating the picture that is to be. Since you don't know what you are making, you have to trust the puzzle maker, believing that what is shown on the box is really the true picture of what all these pieces will look like when you put them together. You have to have confidence that each piece has its place and will fit together perfectly. You know you'll get it sorted out, but it will take time, patience, and—if you're fortunate—some help from friends and family.

I was honored to meet with two beautiful women in their fifties who had lost their husbands to cancer. They were best friends as couples for many years. When the first husband died, the surviving husband of the other couple stepped in and helped his friend's widow sell her house and move to a smaller one. He was the go-to person for his friend's widow as well as for his own precious wife. Then his cancer diagnosis blew a hole in their sense of security. Before long, the two widows were left to grieve together. They never dreamed they would be cast into such an unknown and unwanted season at such a young age.

When I talked with them, they summarized their grief journey with one question: "What just happened?" Their heads were spinning. *How do we do this? How do we get through?* They had to spread the shattered pieces of their lives out on the table and begin to piece together their puzzle of grief. One was two years ahead of the other, but they both had lots of pieces that fit into a similar picture. They both needed answers: What are we going to do? Do we matter anymore? Who are we? Why are we here? Their worlds lay in cut-up pieces that didn't make sense. They needed to find a way and a reason to go on.

As we worked together, piece by piece, we talked about ways to reframe a new picture for each of them. The process didn't change their grief, but it did give them a way to see a new picture of their lives. They had been catapulted out of a season they loved with husbands they adored into a season of widowhood they didn't want and had no idea how to navigate. They understood what grief was, but they needed to put together the pieces of the puzzle to form a picture of who they were. First they had to identify what had just happened and how it was affecting them. They had to examine the puzzle pieces one by one to see how everything fit together. This was their grief work. Failing to do this would have left them sitting at the table, just looking at a bunch of pieces, having no idea what their future picture was going to look like.

The picture they formed was one of service. They found that they needed to be doing something for others who were going through similar pain. Their gifts were in the areas of organization and encouragement, so through their grief work they decided they could offer their services to widows who found themselves in this season of "What just happened?" When someone who understands comes alongside to help sort out the mess, what a difference it can make in moving through grief!

Grief is a burden, but it's also a process. Grief does us no good unless there is an underlying understanding that *someday things will be better*. Grieving is not the goal. Living is the goal. We may grieve what we're leaving behind or what lies ahead, but grieving our lives away is like looking at the pile of puzzle pieces and giving up. *It's too hard. I can't figure it out. I don't have the energy to look at it. I don't want to have to think that hard.* These all are reasons we don't want to work through our grief. I understand, but the day comes when you will either have to work through it or put the lid back on the puzzle box.

Are you facing an unknown season? Are you wondering,

What just happened? Maybe it's time to work through your grief puzzle. Maybe you have courage that you need to tap into as you begin to look at the puzzle pieces in your box.

Maybe this is why I'm writing this book, and maybe this is why you're reading it. Maybe it's really about the grief that change brings even when there are pockets of excitement. Maybe it's realizing there is no change without grief. Maybe it's becoming aware that grief is not just for those who have recently lost a loved one but also for all of us as we move from season to season. No matter if we are happily anticipating what's next or sadly dreading it, we always feel a tinge of pain over leaving behind what has been. That's just who we are. We look back and grieve. We look forward and grieve as well. It's all part of change. And if we live long enough, we can expect many, many changes.

Grief that we feel for these changes can show itself in many forms.

Maybe it's the tear that chokes you as you think about wanting to have one more sunny afternoon playing ball with your beloved dog, now gone.

Or perhaps it's that longing to have your grown children back as little ones for just a day to show them how different a parent you would be now.

Maybe it's the drive by the house where you grew up, thinking, *I'd love to be there for one more night with the family I loved.*

Or it could be the opposite. Maybe you're thinking, *I wish I could spend a night in that house with a family that knew how to love.*

Maybe it's the momentary thought that flashes across your mind as you look at old pictures of the man you married. Although he sits across the room from you now, very much alive, you see those photos and you grieve for that young, fun guy you used to know.

Or perhaps it's the low-grade sorrow you feel as you look at your body. It's been cut up and loaded with chemotherapy. Cancer changed things. You're cancer-free now and you're thankful, but you have gone through trauma that brought grief.

Perhaps it's the deep, silent cry for a mate who never came or a child you never bore or a parent who never loved you. We can all grieve what didn't happen. Even the healthiest of psyches can experience grief for unmet longings of the heart. It doesn't mean that you don't accept God's dealing with you as good. There still can be a wistfulness deep in your soul. It's not overwhelming or part of every day's meditation, but it is there.

All of that is grief—the longing for what was or what could have been.

There are a lot of unknowns and maybes in grief, but every season of life is full of unknowns and maybes because life is full of change and loss.

Look at the following definitions of grief shared by

Russell Friedman. They say it so well. I wonder if these resonate with you like they do with me:

> Grief is the normal and natural emotional reaction to loss or change of any kind. Of itself, grief is neither a pathological condition nor a personality disorder.

> Grief is the conflicting feelings caused by the end of or change in a familiar pattern of behavior.

> Grief is the feeling of reaching out for someone who's always been there, only to discover when I need her [or him] one more time, she's no longer there.

> Grief is the feeling of reaching out for someone who has *never* been there for me, only to discover when I need them one more time, they still aren't there for me.[2]

How do you grieve? What definitions might you use? Can you take parts of these definitions and use them to write out your own definition of grief? Perhaps jot some ideas in the margin of your book and refer back to it from time to time to see how you've changed. Our definitions of grief do change with our experiences. When you come into an unknown season, what happens to you internally? Can you define what you feel?

It's clear: Grief is not a one-size-fits-all emotion. Sometimes we treat each other as if we all should grieve the same. Those of us who have never had a sudden loss with great shock cannot begin to know how long or at what depth a person will experience the waves of grief that wash over them.

Those of you who have always grieved with great emotion cannot begin to understand the less emotional among us. It's such a personal thing.

Those of you who have lost a lifelong mate grieve one way, mourning the loss of a longtime companion.

Those of you whose mate died early in your relationship will grieve another way, grieving for the years of love lost.

Those of you who have just begun to grieve are probably wondering when you will feel like yourself again. No doubt you are full of questions that can't be answered, because everyone goes through grief differently.

If you are grieving a miscarried baby, you grieve in ways no one understands unless it's happened to them.

If you are grieving an adult child, you feel things the parent who lost a ten-year-old won't feel, and yet you both share the painful kinship of children lost.

Those grieving a lost marriage, a friendship betrayed, or a parental rejection have their own ways of grieving.

Loss and change bring grief, and grief will have its way with you. You can't control it. Grief is good, but you won't know the good of it until it's over, and you won't know it's over until you don't feel it anymore. The good news is that you can grieve and at the same time be resilient. You can grieve and be brave. You can grieve and laugh. You can grieve and do many things that seem like a normal part of living. But when you least expect it, a wave of grief will flow over you, and for a moment or for many moments, it will take your breath away. You'll recover. Your brain and body cannot take the intensity of your grief forever. God created us to survive our grief, no matter what we are going through. He made us to be able to grieve and live! We aren't meant to continue to grieve endlessly. Changes come and go, and so does the grief that accompanies the changes in our lives.

Grief and God

If you are a Christ follower, a believer in the One who conquered hell and the grave, then you have a different capacity for grief. We are not immune to changing seasons, to difficult situations, or to deep sorrows that are part of the pangs of life, but believers *will* grieve differently. It's one of the marks of a Christian.

Charles Haddon Spurgeon is known as "the prince of preachers." In October 1856, as Spurgeon was preaching at the Surrey Gardens Music Hall, some people in the crowd yelled, "Fire! The galleries are giving way!" Many people died in a stampede as the crowd panicked and fought to get out. Spurgeon was undone, struggling with depression for many years following the tragic event. He was experiencing grief. So when he wrote the following in *Beside Still Waters*, he knew of what he spoke:

> My dear friend, when grief presses you to the dust, worship there! . . . Remember the exhortation of the Psalmist David, "Pour out your heart before Him; God is a refuge for us" (Ps. 62:8). When you are bowed down beneath a heavy burden of sorrow, worship and adore God there. In full surrender to His divine will, say with Job, "Though He slay me, yet will I trust Him" (Job 13:15). This kind of worship subdues the will, arouses the affections, stirs the whole mind, and presents you to God in solemn consecration. This worship sweetens sorrow and takes away its sting.[3]

The psalmist and repentant sinner King David knew what it was to grieve. Yet in his grieving we see a shining hope. In the dark room of his deepest sorrow, he saw the dawn that would come. The circumstances had been tragic, yet David suffered at his own hand. When kings were supposed to be at war, he was at home with no more to do than to take another man's wife. He saw her; he wanted her; he took her. Then he compounded his sin and sorrow by having her husband killed on the front lines of battle. He thought he had taken care of it all with his clever cover-up, but within a few months it became evident there were things he couldn't cover up. A baby was conceived from this illicit union. *Take the woman for your wife*, he thought. *That will make it all right*. But one day when things had settled down, or at least had seemed to, that pesky prophet Nathan showed up. Tragedy struck David's heart again when Nathan pointed out that God knew about the situation David had tried to cover up and that as a result of his sin and betrayal, the baby would not live. The baby was born and then suffered for seven days before he died.

During that week, David cried out to the Lord for the baby. He fasted and lay all night on the ground. The men of his household stood beside him in order to help, but there was no help for David. He refused their food and their comfort. When the baby died on the seventh day, the men who had stood with David were afraid to tell him because they had seen his despondency when the child was sick. If they had to tell him the baby had died, what would he do? Would he take his own life? They were not sure. As they spoke among themselves as to what to say or do, David heard them and knew that the child had died. He asked, "Is the child dead?" (2 Samuel 12:19). When they fearfully said yes, David did what only a man after God's own heart would do. Even after all the pain and grief he himself had created, David got up from his place of prostration, washed his face, worshiped the Lord, and ate the food that was set before him. David grieved deeply, but his knowledge of the Holy One had eased his sorrow. He was able to go on.

In the midst of the sad scene, David gave the key to why he was able to get up and return to himself in the midst of his great season of disaster. Read it for yourself in 2 Samuel 12:21-23:

> His servants said to him, "What is this thing that you have done? While the child was alive, you fasted and wept; but when the child died, you arose and ate food." He said, "While the child was *still* alive, I fasted and wept; for I said, 'Who knows, the LORD may be gracious to me, that the child may live.' But now he has died; why should I fast? Can I bring him back again? I will go to him, but he will not return to me."

David made a declaration of hope. He believed with all his heart that he would see his son again. He had that much confidence in God—the same God who loved him but who had chastised him for his blatant, rebellious sin. He didn't give up hope because of what he had done. He hoped even more because God had proven Himself true.

That kind of hope didn't rest on something he could

dream up. David knew such hope was worthless. Instead he had hope in the God who had proven Himself over and over even when David had failed miserably. That is true hope. That is God's hope. It covers every loss and change we ever will experience, whether by the will of another person, by our own will, or by the sovereign will of God. There is always hope.

Great Is Thy Faithfulness

God's hope is the key to all that we have talked about as we've journeyed through this book together. As the seasons come and go, hope is what keeps us going. Without hope, we have nothing to look forward to and nothing to sustain us. Hope is the God-factor in every situation. Hope rests on God's promise in Romans 8:28 that through every season and every circumstance, He will cause all things to work together for good for those who love Him and are called according to His purpose.

This is not a promise to just anyone alive but to one who believes in Christ:

> The one who knows that she can't run her own life—but knows God can.
> The one who loves the God she's never seen.
> The one who understands that the same God who spread the stars across the sky knows exactly what she needs.

> The one who knows that God had one Son whom He willingly gave to die on a cross to take her deserved punishment.

If you are in Christ—if you have placed all your trust in Him for your very life and destiny—then you have hope.

If I didn't believe there was hope after this life, there is no way I would look at this last season of my life as anything but a summary. I would just spend time cleaning up and trying to make my exit as pleasant as possible for those I love. I still want to do those things, but the lovely thing is that after our last season on earth, heaven waits. And this is our hope! The day's coming when "He will wipe away every tear from their eyes; and there will no longer be *any* death; there will no longer be *any* mourning, or crying, or pain; the first things have passed away" (Revelation 21:4). And what's more, we will see that our joys and griefs throughout the years were not in vain: God had a plan for us all along. Every season was under His divine control and loving care even though we didn't always feel it. The changes, the losses, the struggles, and the gains were all His way of conforming us to the image of the One He adores, His beloved Son. "We can rejoice, too, when we run into problems and trials, for we know that they help us develop endurance. And endurance develops strength of character, and character strengthens our confident hope of salvation. And this hope will not lead to disappointment. For we know how dearly God loves us, because he has given us the Holy Spirit to fill our hearts with his love" (Romans 5:3-5, NLT).

From my vantage point of looking back over seventy years, I can say living through the seasons has been an adventure. Each had its beauty and fears. Most had moments to remember, and some had moments to forget; yet all made up the sum of my life. I would not be who I am or know what I know had I not lived through each one of those God-given seasons—and neither would you.

My heart cries yes to the words of this woman who wrote by candlelight as she sat out her seventh monsoon:

We all know that if the seasons were the same, there would be no growth. Without winter there would be no spring and without frosts there would be no bulbs and without the monsoon there would be no rice harvest. In the same way we also know that without sorrow there would be no joy. Without pain there would be no healing. I think that's precisely where the beauty comes in. It comes in through the fruit of the seasons. He has indeed made *everything* beautiful in its time.[4]

Indeed, He has. Blessed be His name. And in that beauty we find our lives being lived out with the only

One who can take our sorrow and carve a well of trust so deep in our souls that having known Him only makes us want to know Him more. It is in the looking back that we see His hand and recognize He has been with us all along. From before our conception to this very day, the God of the universe has overseen our lives with love. He has always been faithful.

Scripture tells us that God's love is steadfast and unceasing, and His mercies are new every morning—great is His faithfulness (Lamentations 3:22-23). These words served as the foundation for the famous hymn "Great Is Thy Faithfulness." Following are a few words from that hymn, written by an ordinary man, Thomas Chisholm:

Great is Thy faithfulness!
Morning by morning new mercies I see;
All I have needed Thy hand hath provided—
Great is Thy faithfulness, Lord, unto me!

Born in a log cabin in Franklin, Kentucky, Chisholm became a Christian when he was twenty-seven and entered the ministry when he was thirty-six, though poor health forced him to retire after just one year. During the rest of his life, Chisholm spent many years living in New Jersey and working as a life insurance agent. . . .

Chisholm explained toward the end of his life, "My income has not been large at any time due to impaired health in the earlier years which has followed me on until now. Although I must not fail to record here the unfailing faithfulness of a covenant-keeping God and that He has given me many wonderful displays of His providing care, for which I am filled with astonishing gratefulness."[5]

"Morning by morning new mercies I see"—He's always been there, and He's never failed to be faithful.

Those of us who can look back on the many years of the seasons we've already lived can say, "Yes, it's all true. He's been ever so faithful to me." I was told that on her deathbed my mother, though she had not spoken for several days, reached her hand toward heaven and said, "Thank You, Lord, for always taking care of me. Thank You, Lord, for always being there." She dropped her hand, and in a few minutes she raised it again and said, "I see, I see!" When asked what she saw, she didn't answer, for at that moment she had breathed her last on earth. Her final season was finished.

The God my mother thanked for caring for her all those years ago is still the same today. He will be the same God tomorrow. Whatever comes next, He will be there.

This beautiful prayer of Francis de Sales is my prayer

for you as you move into whatever unknown season waits in your life:

PRAYER OF ST. FRANCIS DE SALES

Be at Peace
Do not look forward in fear to the changes of life;
rather look to them with full hope as they arise.
God, whose very own you are,
will deliver you from out of them.
He has kept you hitherto,
and He will lead you safely through all things;
and when you cannot stand it,
God will bury you in His arms.
Do not fear what may happen tomorrow;
the same everlasting Father who cares for you today
will take care of you then and every day.
He will either shield you from suffering,
or will give you unfailing strength to bear it.
Be at peace,
and put aside all anxious thoughts and imagination.[6]

Notes

CHAPTER ONE: SEASONS COME AND SEASONS GO

1. This is not a hard, firm fact but a general approximation for the sake of discussion.
2. December 7 may not call a particular event to mind for centennials (those born after the year 2000), but for the silent generation it is a day that will live in infamy. Similarly, the assassination of John F. Kennedy was an event that defined the baby boomers more than any other, and millennials quickly recall where they were when terrorists flew airplanes into the twin towers of the World Trade Center.
3. Martha T. S. Laham, "THIS Is Really When Old Age Begins," *Huffington Post*, September 14, 2015, accessed March 29, 2017, http://www .huffingtonpost.com/martha-ts-laham-/when-old-age-begins_b_8099004 .html.
4. Elisabeth Elliot, "Restlessness and Worry," *The Elisabeth Elliot Newsletter*, September/October 2003, accessed March 29, 2017, http://www .elisabethelliot.org/newsletters/2003-09-10.pdf.
5. Kay Arthur, *When the Hurt Runs Deep: Healing and Hope for Life's Desperate Moments* (Colorado Springs: WaterBrook, 2010), 29.

CHAPTER TWO: RESILIENCE

1. "FYI: Building Your Resilience," APA Practice Organization, accessed March 23, 2017, http://www.apapracticecentral.org/outreach/building -resilience.aspx.
2. Dan Baker, *What Happy People Know: How the New Science of Happiness Can Change Your Life for the Better* (New York: St. Martin's Press, 2003), 123.
3. Nathan Furr, "How Failure Taught Edison to Repeatedly Innovate," *Forbes*, June 9, 2011, accessed March 29, 2017, https://www.forbes.com/sites /nathanfurr/2011/06/09/how-failure-taught-edison-to-repeatedly-innovate /#4cc7ff7465e9.

4. Christopher Reeve, in Oliver Burkeman, "Man of Steel," *The Guardian*, September 17, 2002, accessed March 23, 2017, https://www.theguardian .com/education/2002/sep/17/science.highereducation.

5. Maia Szalavitz, "Q&A: Positive Psychologist Martin Seligman on the Good Life," *Time*, May 13, 2011, http://healthland.time.com/2011/05/13/mind -reading-positive-psychologist-martin-seligman-on-the-good-life/.

6. Helen McIntosh, e-mail to the author, July 2016. Used with permission.

7. Jenny Suddeth, e-mail to the author, July 2016. Used with permission.

8. Joseph Benson, *The Holy Bible, Containing the Old and New Testaments*, Volume 2 (New York: G. Lane & C. B. Tippett, 1846), 736.

CHAPTER THREE: FIGHT FEAR

1. I heard Chuck say this at lunch one day.

2. Ravi Zacharias, *Cries of the Heart: Bringing God Near When He Feels So Far* (Nashville: Thomas Nelson, 2002), 24.

3. Dr. Michael L. Williams, "What Is a Prayer of Supplication? A Christian Study," What Christians Want to Know, accessed March 23, 2017, http:// www.whatchristianswanttoknow.com/what-is-a-prayer-of-supplication.

4. Dan Baker, *What Happy People Know: How the New Science of Happiness Can Change Your Life for the Better* (New York: St. Martin's Press, 2003), 79, 81.

5. Augustine of Hippo, *Confessions*, trans. F. J. Sheed (Indianapolis: Hackett, 2006), 3.

CHAPTER FOUR: DON'T FORGET TO LAUGH

1. Abraham Lincoln, quoted in Merrill D. Johnson, *Lincoln in American Memory* (New York: Oxford University Press, 1994), 97.

2. Viktor E. Frankl, *Man's Search for Meaning* (Boston: Beacon Press, 2006), 44.

3. Dr. Dacher Keltner in Linda Graham, "Laughter," *Wise Brain Bulletin*, vol. 3.8, August 2009, accessed April 3, 2017, http://lindagraham-mft.net /resources/published-articles/laughter/.

4. "A Merry Heart or a Broken Spirit," GodSaidManSaid, accessed March 23, 2017, https://www.godsaidmansaid.com/topic3.asp?Cat1=81&Cat2 =244&ItemId=687; see also Nicholas Plotnikoff, Anthony Murgo, Robert Faith, and Joseph Wybran, *Stress and Immunity* (Boca Raton, FL: CRC Press, 1991), 169; Norman B. Anderson, ed., *Encyclopedia of Health and Behavior* (Thousand Oaks, CA: Sage Publications, 2004), 50; and Richard Gray, "Grief Leaves the Body at Risk of Infection," *Telegraph*, March 25, 2012, accessed March 23, 2017, http://www.telegraph.co.uk/news/health /news/9164466/Grief-leaves-the-body-at-risk-of-infection.html.

5. Ibid.
6. Ibid.; see also Anita V. Clark, ed., *Psychology of Moods* (New York: Nova Science Publishers, Inc., 2005), 53.
7. "Hospice Dog Tenderly Comforts Dying Patient," YouTube video, 1:16, posted by *USA Today*, August 25, 2015, accessed March 23, 2017, https://www.youtube.com/watch?v=zO9WfW5ZvZ0.

CHAPTER FIVE: WHY NOT?
1. Ellie Lofaro, e-mail to author, March 2017. Used with permission.
2. Bob Lowry, "What Will I Be Doing When I Turn 70? Probably Not What I Am Doing Today," *70 Things to Do When You Turn 70*, ed. Ronnie Sellers (South Portland, ME: Sellers Publishing, 2013), 70.
3. Grandma Moses, *Grandma Moses: My Life's History* (New York: Harper & Brothers, 1952), n.p.
4. Grandma Moses in Bill Swainson, ed., *Encarta Book of Quotations* (New York: St. Martin's Press, 2000), 389.
5. Grandma Moses, quoted in Louise Matteoni, *New Leaves* (New York: Economy, 1986), n.p.
6. Patsy's paintings are for sale on the Internet. Check them out at Rosecreek Road: Patsy's Studio, accessed March 29, 2017, http://www.rosecreekroad.com.
7. To learn more about Phoebe Snetsinger, read her memoir, *Birding on Borrowed Time* (Delaware City, DE: American Birding Association, 2003).

CHAPTER SIX: LETTING GO
1. Don Wyrtzen, "Finally Home" (New Spring, 1971).
2. Story used with permission.
3. Gloria Gaither, interview by Stephen Hubbard and Scott Ross, "God's 'Interruption' of the Gaithers," CBN, accessed March 23, 2017, http://www.cbn.com/cbnmusic/interviews/700club_gaithers0805.aspx?mobile=false.
4. Brother Lawrence, *The Practice of the Presence of God: The Wisdom and Teachings of Brother Lawrence*, compiled by Father Joseph de Beaufort (Wildside Press, 2010), 5.

CHAPTER SEVEN: HEAD TOWARD NINETY
1. "Pain Medicines (Analgesics)," National Kidney Foundation, accessed March 29, 2017, https://www.kidney.org/atoz/content/painmeds_analgesics.
2. Eunyoung Cho, ScD; Gary Curhan, MD, ScD; Susan E. Hankinson, ScD; et al., "Prospective Evaluation of Analgesic Use and Risk of Renal Cell

Cancer," *JAMA Internal Medicine*, September 12, 2011, accessed March 29, 2017, http://jamanetwork.com/journals/jamainternalmedicine /fullarticle/1106087?resultClick=1.

3. Beverly Merz, "Common anticholinergic drugs like Benadryl linked to increased dementia risk," *Harvard Health Publications*, January 28, 2015, accessed March 29, 2017, http://www.health.harvard.edu/blog/common -anticholinergic-drugs-like-benadryl-linked-increased-dementia-risk -201501287667.

4. While some insomnia is normal, don't let chronic, persistent insomnia go on too long. For some (nonmedical) treatment proposals that can help you navigate chronic insomnia, see https://www.ncbi.nlm.nih.gov/pmc /articles/PMC2924526/.

5. "How Much Sugar Do You Eat? You May Be Surprised!" New Hampshire Department of Health and Human Services, accessed March 29, 2017, http://www.dhhs.nh.gov/dphs/nhp/documents/sugar.pdf.

6. Michael Hawthorne, "Mercury in Corn Syrup? Food Made with Ingredient May Have Traces of Toxic Metal," *Chicago Tribune*, January 27, 2009, accessed March 29, 2017, http://www.chicagotribune.com/lifestyles/chi -mercury-corn-syrupjan27-story.html.

7. Lynne Terry, "High-Fructose Corn Syrup More Toxic Than Sugar, Study Finds," *Oregonian*, January 5, 2015, accessed March 23, 2017, http:// www.oregonlive.com/health/index.ssf/2015/01/high-fructose_corn_syrup _more.html.

8. "Calcium Supplements May Damage the Heart," Johns Hopkins Medicine, October 11, 2016, accessed March 23, 2017, http://www.hopkinsmedicine .org/news/media/releases/calcium_supplements_may_damage_the_heart.

CHAPTER EIGHT: WHAT ABOUT THE CHILDREN?

1. Claire Berman, "What Aging Parents Want from Their Kids," *Atlantic*, March 4, 2016, accessed March 23, 2017, https://www.theatlantic.com /health/archive/2016/03/when-youre-the-aging-parent/472290/.

2. Courtland Milloy, "Watching Out for Aging Parents," *Washington Post*, September 3, 2013, accessed March 23, 2017, https://www .washingtonpost.com/local/watching-out-for-aging-parents/2013/09 /03/0774add4-14cc-11e3-a100-66fa8fd9a50c_story.html?utm_term =.f13206b45ffa.

3. Howard Gleckman, "The Worst Advice for Family Caregivers: Parent Your Aging Parents," September 4, 2013, accessed March 23, 2017, http://www.forbes.com/sites/howardgleckman/2013/09/04/the-worst -advice-for-family-caregivers-parent-your-aging-parents/#2b8d4d635a24.

4. Sam Hamstra, Jr., "Honor," in *Baker's Evangelical Dictionary of Biblical Theology*, ed. Walter A. Elwell (Grand Rapids, MI: Baker), accessed March 23, 2017, http://www.biblestudytools.com/dictionaries/bakers-evangelical -dictionary/honor.html.

5. Bob Deffinbaugh, "Between Child and Parent—Honoring Father and Mother (Exodus 20:12)," Bible.org, accessed March 28, 2017, https://bible .org/seriespage/18-between-child-and-parent-honoring-father-and-mother -exodus-2012.

CHAPTER NINE: CLEAN UP AFTER YOURSELF

1. Please check out the National Association of Senior Move Managers (NASMM) at http://www.nasmm.org (accessed March 28, 2017). NASMM is a nonprofit association supporting more than five hundred senior move professionals throughout the United States and Canada. A professional move manager helps older adults and families with the physical and emotional tasks associated with later-life transitions, including death.

2. Story used with permission.

3. See the website Leave Nothing Unsaid, accessed May 7, 2017, http:// www.LeaveNothingUnsaid.com.

4. Jody Noland, "About the Program," Leave Nothing Unsaid, accessed May 12, 2017, www.leavenothingunsaid.com/about.

CHAPTER TEN: GRIEF AND HOPE

1. "Grief," Online Etymology Dictionary, accessed March 28, 2017, http:// www.etymonline.com/index.php?term=grief&allowed_in_frame=0.

2. Russell Friedman, "The Best Grief Definition You Will Find," *The Grief Recovery Method* (blog), June 4, 2013, accessed March 28, 2017, http://blog.griefrecoverymethod.com/blog/2013/06/best-grief-definition -you-will-find.

3. Charles Spurgeon, *Beside Still Waters* (Nashville: Thomas Nelson, 1999), n.p.

4. Naomi Reed, *My Seventh Monsoon: A Himalayan Journey of Faith and Mission* (Milton Keynes, UK: Authentic Media, 2011), n.p.

5. "'Great Is Thy Faithfulness'—The Story behind the Hymn," Gaither, accessed March 23, 2017, http://www.gaither.com/news/"great-thy -faithfulness"-story-behind-hymn.

6. "Prayer of St. Francis de Sales," in Dr. Benjamin Mast, *Second Forgetting* (Grand Rapids, MI: Zondervan, 2014), n.p.

More Praise for *Courage for the Unknown Season*

It is one thing to have a trusted counselor help you prepare for seasons to come, but it's quite another to have a good friend grab your hand and say to you, "I know you can handle whatever lies ahead." Jan comes alongside us all, no matter what season of life we're currently in, and helps us prepare for one of the surest aspects of life: change. With her love of Scripture, hard-won wisdom, and empathetic heart, Jan brings a clear-eyed view of some of the difficulties change brings in tow, but also helps us recognize the beautiful opportunities each season presents. This book is a toolbox, a road map, and an invitation to live with tenacity and grace.

ANITA RENFROE
Comedian

The words and wisdom of Jan Silvious have a way of comforting us into courage—of prodding us into the many uncharted territories of living through the hope of a big-picture faith. Even with life's seismic shifts, Jan's words encourage us that life is worth living.

ANDREW GREER
Singer-songwriter and author

We all need a friend to come alongside us at times of new adventures and new seasons. Jan Silvious is just such a friend.

JAN PETERSON
Author

No matter how long we live in this skin, we will experience seasons. Some will crown us; some will challenge us. But with a little faith in God and a lot of good advice from Jan, our mountains will become molehills, and we will be laughing with life again.

MARK LOWRY
Singer-songwriter and comedian